The Freedom From Depression WORKBOOK

The Freedom From Depression WORKBOOK

Les Carter Ph.D. | **Frank Minirth** M.D.

A JANET THOMA BOOK

THOMAS NELSON PUBLISHERS
Nashville

Published in Nashville, Tennessee, by Thomas Nelson, Inc., Publishers, and distributed in Canada by Word Communications, Ltd., Richmond, British Columbia.

The Bible version used in this publication is THE NEW KING JAMES VERSION. Copyright © 1979, 1980, 1982, 1990, Thomas Nelson, Inc., Publishers.

ISBN 0–8407-6207-0

Printed in the United States of America.

1 2 3 4 5 6 — 00 99 98 97 96 95

Dedicated to our fellow workers at the
Minirth Meier New Life Clinics
who are dedicated to the team approach
in treating emotional and mental disorders.

How necessary and appreciated you are!

Contents

Preface

A high-powered businessman once said, "Fortunately, I'll never have to worry about being depressed. I've never experienced it because my personality is not bent that way." About two years later this man became a patient at our clinic . . . his diagnosis—major depression, acute episode. In the time following his bold statement he had experienced a series of losses that emotionally weighed him down as never before. Upon completion of his treatment he recalled his earlier words and said, "If someone like me could become depressed, it could happen to anyone."

How correct this man was! Depression does not play favorites. You may be an introvert or extrovert, socially active or shy, youthful or elderly, male or female, wealthy or poor, white-collar or blue-collar, religious or secular. Whatever your distinction, you can also become depressed. What is more, any person you know is likewise fair game.

As practitioners in the field of psychiatry and counseling, we each ceased being surprised years ago at how commonly depression can invade the lives of the patients who come to our clinic. We try to be sensitive to the fact that most of these people—like the businessman—never thought they would be laid low by this problem. They naturally question: "How could this happen to me? Is there a way out?"

We are very staunch in the conviction that depression does not have to be terminal. It is not so mysterious that it defies explanations and solutions. If you are a depressed person, proceed with hope.

Now can be a time of serious personal reflection regarding the experiences and trends that have brought this emotional intrusion into your life. As you read, know that the two most important ingredients in your growth are an inquisitive mind and a willingness to challenge the ways of responding to problems. You *can* be helped!

If you are a friend or loved one of someone experiencing depression, thanks for caring enough to learn about this problem so you can be part of the solution. Know that your consistent encouragement and understanding can go a long way toward helping someone else find the optimism that can lift that person from his or her current low moods.

We have tried to keep our discussion of depression uncomplicated and pertinent. Instead of academically presenting the facts and insights we have gleaned through our years of practice, we have settled upon the workbook format for a very specific reason. We want you to personalize the information so you can see for yourself that depression does not have to claim you as a permanent victim.

Ponder the checklists carefully and respond thoughtfully to the questions. You may decide to share your responses with a trusted friend, your minister, or a professional counselor. Perhaps you will use the workbook as part of a larger class or support group. Allowing others to know about your situation can help the healing process and can create a much-needed sense of community and accountability.

You will notice that we have included real-life illustrations of people who have struggled, like you, to find freedom from depression. Know that for confidentiality reasons we have altered identifying elements of the persons involved. But also know that we included their stories to let you see that you are not alone.

Don't expect an easy way out of this unwanted malady. But don't despair either. Each chapter can cause new awarenesses and can give new ideas about how you can peel back the layers of your situation and come to terms with this emotion.

Our prayers and hopes are with you! Brighter days are ahead!

Acknowledgments

Special thanks are extended to Irene Swindell, Carol Mandt, and Ann Jensly for their assistance in preparing the manuscript.

We are also indebted to the staff at Thomas Nelson Publishers, especially Janet Thoma and Emily Kirkpatrick for their expertise in readying the manuscript for publication.

To our wives, Mary Alice Minirth and Leigh Ann Carter, we are grateful for your daily support and your ongoing interest in our vital work with depressed patients.

The case illustrations in this book are composite renderings of people we have had the privilege of treating through the years. We genuinely enjoy our work and we gain tremendous inspiration from our many patients who have given us reason to have hope and optimism, in spite of the presence of very real problems in our lives.

Twelve Steps to Managing Depression

Step 1. Be aware of the indicators that tell you that changes are needed.

Step 2. Know that anger can be uncovered and choices can be made regarding its purpose.

Step 3. Become committed to healthy boundaries and assertions.

Step 4. Believe in yourself. Know your worth and value as a person.

Step 5. Refuse to be a perpetual victim of past or present abuse.

Step 6. Allow time for natural grief to run its course.

Step 7. Know that the best way to be in control is to resist the craving to be in control.

Step 8. Make allowances for painful truths.

Step 9. Understand how your personality can predispose you to depressive feelings.

Step 10. Be open-minded as you consider the medical aspects of depression.

Step 11. Reveal your struggles with thoughts about death. Allow others to know you thoroughly.

Step 12. Be committed to positive attitudes that can bring balance to your emotions.

1

You Can Identify
Your Depression

Step 1. Be aware of the indicators that tell you
that changes are needed.

"From what you're telling me," said Dr. Carter, "you seem to be
experiencing an ongoing depression." Across from him sat Janice, a
professional woman in her mid-forties who had been describing
years of hidden frustrations. Her face, which in the past had radiated
joy and enthusiasm, now appeared numb and defeated. It had been
months since she had laughed out loud. She cried easily and admitted she was having difficulty figuring out how she had fallen into
such a hole.

"I know you're probably right," she sighed. Then speaking slowly
she explained, "I hate admitting that I could be so far into my sour
feelings that I'd be labeled as clinically depressed. Just the word,
depression, sounds so ugly, so final. What puzzles me is that I have
no real history of depression, at least not like I'm feeling right now."

She shook her head as she elaborated, "I've felt down and discouraged about things before, but I've always been able to bounce back. Somehow it seems different now. Even small problems become big ones. Just last night my husband had to cancel some evening plans with me because of an unexpected problem at work. In the past I would have just shrugged it off, but when I hung up the phone I started crying. Do you remember the cartoon character with the rain cloud constantly overhead? That's what I feel like, but really, this just isn't me!"

This just isn't me. How often do we hear those words when persons describe the depression they feel? More accurately, people like Janice are *really* saying, "This is a part of me I would like to be rid of forever."

Janice's depression had been quietly building for years. After earning her college degree more than twenty years ago she had determined to take the world by storm. Always the confident one, she had climbed the ladder of success in the banking industry and had developed a solid reputation that served her well. Even when changes caused colleagues to worry about keeping their jobs, she had never lost a night's sleep worrying about her career. "The world of banking has been volatile," she explained, "but I'm a survivor who's weathered mergers and buyouts well." Because she had always seemed so invulnerable no one would guess it was her secret struggle with insecurity and performance pressure that had pushed her to be a notch above the rest.

On the surface, Janice seemed to have the all-American life. But in her counseling she eventually learned that the most important elements for emotional stability were those beneath the surface . . . and that was a different story.

Both parents had died by the time she was twenty-five, so they missed the chance to meet her eventual husband and daughter. She had a sister who lived nearby, and they were committed to keeping family traditions alive, even if it was just the two of them. Best friends, they often reminisced fondly about their early years with parents who took the time to listen and encourage. They recalled together how their mother in particular was funny and eager to entertain Janice's friends in their home. Dad was the quiet type who rarely shared his deepest feelings. A successful businessman, he exuded confidence; and, despite his closed communication, no one doubted his love and support.

Marrying in her late twenties, Janice had now been with Wayne sixteen years. Their relationship had never been storybook perfect, they often would go weeks without meaningful conversation. But they didn't have an awful relationship either. They fought infrequently and were fairly similar in their methods of raising their daughter, Sarah, who was now twelve. Popular at school and involved in sports, Sarah kept her mother busy as they coordinated schedules so she would suffer few ill effects of having a working mom. Motivated by the memories of the good times spent with her own mother, Janice openly encouraged Sarah to talk freely about her friends, needs, and dreams. She was a good parent.

Likewise, Janice had a satisfactory social life. Active in church, she had numerous friends and acquaintances who were available for dinners and other outings. And though her professional schedule prohibited her from participating in many weekday activities, she and Wayne put high priority on their social contacts so they would never feel their lives were too one-dimensional.

So where was the depression coming from?

First, let's acknowledge that depression does not just befall weak and problem-prone people. If you ever assume that you can be immune from experiencing this condition, think again. Given the right ingredients anyone can suffer from depression. Cold facts tell us that at any given time 5 to 10 percent of Americans currently feel depressed. Over the course of a lifetime 20 to 25 percent will experience strong bouts of depression, and many of these people will seriously contemplate taking their own lives. And even if you never become seriously depressed, virtually each person is assured of periodic struggles with discouragement and defeat. Depression is symptomatic of life in an imperfect, fallen world, and it plays no favorites with race, creed, or color.

In the case of Janice, several factors became apparent as she and Dr. Carter explored the reasons for her depression. Being an achiever who insisted on keeping a clean image, Janice habitually downplayed her insecurities and needs. "I'll handle it myself" was her motto. Her good sense of pride and self-reliance sometimes boomeranged and became her own worst enemy. She hated appearing weak.

This led to a further problem of suppressing her emotions. For instance, if she felt hurt because of a colleague's cutting remark she would think, "I can't let this person get the best of me." If she felt needy because she and Wayne had shared little closeness, she would reason, "I don't want to appear clingy." If she was tired when asked to attend a committee meeting she would nonetheless reply, "Sure, what time does it start?" She just *had* to appear strong, no matter the immediate cost. Can you relate?

With this suppressing style of handling emotions came a further problem: building anger. Not one to shout or raise a ruckus, she hesitated to describe herself as angry. Yet, she would quickly admit that she was frequently frustrated and increasingly resentful. Anxiety mounted as she attempted to keep up her veneer, so she had become more defensive and cautious in communicational patterns. Edginess thus increased.

Do you see the pattern of downward spiraling? Rather than slamming you to the floor suddenly, depression tends to creep up on you gradually. As in Janice's case, it is usually the result of long-standing patterns of communications and emotional management that, taken to an extreme, can wear you down.

What has been your experience? As you examine your relationship patterns from years past, what two or three trends do you notice that have led to increased frustration with life? (For instance, "I have a hard time telling people how hurt I really feel," or "I cannot forgive some people for past abuse.")

1. _____

_____

2. _____

_____

3. _____

_____

To minimize the effects of depression in your life, you must first recognize what it is and how it got there. No simple task, you must be willing to be honest about your needs and weaknesses.

To determine your potential vulnerability to depression, check the following items that apply to you:

— I feel sad or discouraged more than I would like.

— It is easy to dwell on what might go wrong. I can be pessimistic.

— Socially, I would prefer to withdraw rather than to be in groups.

— I have a low interest these days in sexual activity.

— Others might describe me as moody or irritable.

— I have regrets about the past that will not fade easily.

— Sometimes I struggle with feelings of inadequacy and low self-esteem.

— There have been times recently when the thought of dying has seemed appealing.

— Laughter and joviality do not come as naturally as they once did.

— My sleep patterns have been irregular; either I want to sleep too much or I cannot sleep enough.

— My appetite has changed; I eat either too much or too little.

— I cannot seem to sustain my motivation to complete tasks.

___ My concentration level is just not what it should be.

___ I cannot seem to get over feelings of grief or loss.

___ I feel on the verge of crying more than I normally should be.

___ Recently I've been thinking more about things I resent.

___ I find it hard to be fully open in disclosing my deepest feelings and needs.

___ Lately I have felt trapped by a sense of duty and obligation.

___ I have had a hard time handling feelings of rejection or abandonment.

___ I am not really sure that many people would care if I told them how I feel.

How many items did you check? Keep in mind it would be abnormal *not* to respond to some of these items. If you responded to five or fewer, you could be inclined toward such a free-spirited life that you do not allow yourself to be honest about your hurts. If you responded to between six and ten items, you could have stretches of time when depression has a hold on you, yet you can also be expected to interact normally with your world much of the time. If you responded to between eleven and fifteen items, you are quite susceptible to a major depression. Don't take your situation lightly. You will need to explore your feelings and lifestyle habits with someone (probably a professional) who can help you get on track with more successful strategies for handling your many tensions. If you checked sixteen or more, you definitely should seek help. In addition to counseling, you should get a full medical evaluation. There is hope for you; do not let your patterns become so entrenched that they rob you of your will to live.

Defining Depression

The word *depression* can mean different things to different people. Some use it so commonly that they relate it to being disappointed or hurt or discouraged, often by minor problems. When others use it they describe themselves as feeling so debilitated by life that they can hardly function.

A good working definition of depression would be a feeling of sadness and dejection resulting in an increasingly pessimistic outlook on life. Included in depression can be a mental dullness as demonstrated by poor concentration and a breakdown in reasoning abilities. It is usually accompanied by such symptoms as social withdrawal, decreased motivation, lessened sex drive (or conversely a willingness toward normally unthinkable immorality), sleep disturbances, increased anxiety, edginess, and critical thoughts.

Looking back over this definition and examining your responses to the inventory, what would you say are your most common indicators of depression?

1. _____
2. _____
3. _____
4. _____

Some people, like Janice, make matters worse because they have an aversion to calling depression by its name. They participate in a form of denial. Janice was so busy trying to maintain such a correct image that she had unwittingly convinced herself that she would lose status if she admitted weaknesses or needs. Not only could she not let others believe she had problems, she would not let herself believe it. To be depressed meant that she could not make the grade, and she was so intent on being above common problems that she would not even allow herself to question why she felt unstable.

She confessed to Dr. Carter, "I can now look back ten years and see how I've been struggling in some way or another with many of my symptoms. I distinctly remember, though, when a colleague of mine was actually hospitalized for depression. The news of this spread around the office very quickly and soon everyone knew he'd experienced a nervous breakdown."

Nodding, Dr. Carter injected, "So you determined then and there that you couldn't afford to be similarly labeled, right?"

Speaking carefully, she explained, "My world is very cutthroat, and the main difference between those who make it and those who don't is that the survivors never let on that they are really mortal. There's always someone who would love to replace you, so you have to be above human frailties."

Another problem that could keep you from disclosing depression is that others have no clue about how to respond to your feelings, so you avoid discussions about them, knowing others will just tell you how to solve your problem quickly. For instance, Janice told Dr. Carter, "Not too long ago I felt I had to tell my secretary about my problem because she was becoming curious about my appointments I made each week away from the office. As soon as I said I had been depressed she went on about how her sister had experienced the same thing and then she began giving me advice about how I could change my life for the better."

"How did you react when she talked with you about this?"

"Well, I was more turned off than anything else," she said. "I didn't tell her about my depression so she could give me advice. All I wanted was her tolerance and understanding, but I don't think she can appreciate how helpful that would be. The more she talked, the less I wanted to reveal about myself."

Keeping in mind that depression is worsened by an ongoing habit of suppressing emotions, it is clear to see that people like Janice face a real dilemma. Do they tell people about their problems, knowing it may cause more frustration than they want or need? Do they continue to hold in their feelings even though it requires maintaining a facade?

Perhaps you have never been under the same business pressures as Janice, but maybe you too can recall how risky it might be to refer openly to your problem with depression. So you cover up.

What pressures have you faced that have inhibited you from admitting the extent of your depressed feelings? (For instance, "My family has always been critical of weak people," or "I'm in leadership positions and can't afford to let my guard down.")

1. _____
   _____

2. _____
   _____

To make strides toward remedying your depression, you will need to be honest about it to as many people as common sense would allow. Keeping your problems hidden will only worsen your feelings since depression by definition is usually the result of unaddressed emotions.

Talking openly with Dr. Carter about her symptoms was a major first step for Janice. "I've always thought I would feel ashamed if I had to admit being depressed," she confessed. "But right now I'm more relieved that it is out in the open. Maybe I've made my problem worse by being too proud or self-protective, so I guess you could say it's about time I learned from my mistakes. I want to be less guarded."

"No doubt, you've done yourself a favor by pulling back your curtains," said the doctor. "Perhaps you'll be able to find someone outside the counseling office who can be trusted with your feelings. In the weeks ahead we'll need to build on your openness by exploring the underlying causes and cures for your depression."

Can you, too, speak of your depression openly as you commit to resolving it? What would be different in your life if you did? (For instance, "I would apologize to my friends less when I expose a need," or "I'd let a coworker know that I'm getting professional help.")

_____

_____

_____

Before we move on, let's also recognize that depression can be a by-product of other physical or medical problems. As we assess patients for depression we check for several biological factors that can explain the downward shift in mood. For instance:

• Have you had major surgery in the past year?

• Have you had a history of cardiac problems, or are you in a high-risk group for heart problems (heavy smoker, overweight, etc.)?

• Do you suffer from ongoing physical discomfort caused by a chronic disorder such as rheumatoid arthritis?

• Are you taking birth control pills?

• Have you had recent problems with your gastrointestinal system?

• Do you suffer from abdominal pain, headaches, backaches, or chest pains?

• Have you been taking medicines that have known side effects of sedation or excitability?

- Do you regularly use alcohol, marijuana, or other mood-enhancing drugs?

- Is there a history of liver or kidney disease in your family?

- Do you experience an eating disorder (anorexic habits, purging, binge eating, etc.)?

- Do you have chronic sinus problems requiring frequent use of decongestant medicines?

- Are you taking blood pressure medicines, diuretics, or major pain relievers?

- Have you suffered from a major viral infection such as mononucleosis or pneumonia?

- Have you been diagnosed with an endocrine disorder such as hypothyroidism or Cushing's syndrome?

- Do you have a major disease such as Alzheimer's disease, multiple sclerosis, lupus, cancer, Parkinson's disease, or muscular dystrophy?

- Have you suspected the growth of tumors or have you had a recent head trauma?

- Have you ever been diagnosed with epilepsy?

- Have you been treated in the past year with steroids?

This series of questions is not exhaustive, but it demonstrates that depression is often linked to factors other than just emotional stress.

When we learn that a physiological problem is strongly featured in a person's struggle with depression, we will insist first that it be given due attention before proceeding with the typical psychotherapeutic approach of treatment. Understand, psychotherapy is usually very necessary in treating depression, but it can often stall if underlying physical problems are not resolved.

What medical or physiological problems have you experienced that could potentially factor into your experience of depression?

1. _____

2. _____

3. _____

4. _____

In the year prior to counseling, Janice had major physical problems that eventually required back surgery. She explained to Dr. Carter, "Several years ago I injured my back in a serious snow skiing accident. We tried physical therapy for a long time, but last year my doctor finally had to perform surgery. I still have pain that keeps me from sitting still for long periods of time, but then I also hurt if I'm on my feet too long. It's a no-win situation."

"Do you take prescription medicines to relieve the pain?"

"Sometimes. For a while my doctor prescribed some muscle relaxants, but they didn't really help much. So now I keep a prescription painkiller in the medicine cabinet. I try not to take them often, but when the pain gets bad I've just got to take one for some relief."

Dr. Carter realized that chronic pain can seriously inhibit emotional well-being, and he also knew that her medicines could easily alter moods. So he explained, "We can't assume that your medical problem is the complete cause for your depression, but it would be very safe to say it is an ongoing contributor."

Problems like Janice's should never be considered lightly. Your emotional system is strongly influenced by your bodily health. Sometimes depression can be the direct result of medical treatments, as in the case of heart disease or cancer, meaning the depression should be understood within the context of that illness. Other times, as in the case of Janice's bad back, the depression is not directly caused by a physical problem, but it is a major factor nonetheless. Make sure your doctor knows about all such symptoms as you are in the diagnostic process.

Finally, as your depression is being diagnosed, be aware of the role of major stressors or life adjustments. Most people (even those who consider themselves free spirits) like a degree of predictability or familiarity in their lives. But sometimes changes or tragedies occur that throw us completely out of our comfort zones, causing susceptibility to depression.

For instance, some of the most common stressors that can propel you headlong into depression could include the following:

- death in the family or death of a close friend

- major career change, especially if it is a setback

- divorce or marital separation

- personal injury or prolonged illness

- major legal problems

- loss of financial stability, such as bankruptcy or income tax problems

- long-standing, seemingly unresolvable, marital problems

- inability to feel that you've found your niche in your circle of acquaintances or in the community

- moving from one city to another

- ongoing strains with children

- day-by-day strain of living with one or more toddlers in the home

- infidelity discovered in the marriage

- battles with alcohol or drugs

- chronic conflict with coworkers or supervisors; job dissatisfaction

- loss of close friendship, especially if it involved a clear rejection

- living through retirement with little stimulating activity

- the "empty-nest" syndrome

Any one of these problems can thrust a person into depression, with it being compounded when you experience multiple stressors at the same time. You may normally have good coping skills, yet you can learn just how limited you are when you try to make sense of unexpected or unwanted circumstances that strain those skills to the max.

What major stressors have you experienced within the past two or three years?

1. _____
2. _____
3. _____
4. _____

As you have been influenced by these stressors, what changes have you noticed in your personality? (For instance, "I am more noticeably discouraged," or "I don't initiate contact with any friends like I used to.")

1. _____
2. _____
3. _____
4. _____

As you can tell by the information in just this first chapter, depression can show itself in many ways and can arise for many reasons. But hold on to optimism! Depression can be managed.

When you seek treatment, you may be encouraged to use a pharmacological approach (antidepressant medicines). Such treatment is not for everyone, but some cannot progress without it. Under psychological and relational stress, the body often fails to function at its full capacity. Stress can deplete the neurotransmitters in the brain (serotonin, norepinephrine, dopamine), which in turn produces depression. Stress can also slow the recovery from diseases and surgery, thus leaving a person more vulnerable to depression.

Usually doctors can tell if medical intervention is needed when the patient persistently suffers from the symptoms of sleep disruption, morning blues, crying spells, appetite changes, thoughts of suicide, extreme sluggishness, feelings of hopelessness, or physical symptoms such as migraine headaches.

In some cases, medicine is the only way to relieve depressive features. For example, when a bipolar (manic-depressive) disorder is diagnosed, the symptoms usually will not abate until medicines are introduced. Other diagnoses that would necessitate a medical approach would include psychotic depressive reaction and schizophrenic disorder. If your depression includes symptoms indicating you are losing touch with reality or are acting severely out of character, be certain that disorders of this type are ruled out first by a competent psychiatrist or medical doctor thoroughly familiar with these problems.

Should you be given careful advice to use antidepressants, be willing to make good use of them. Too commonly we hear people protest: "Using antidepressants means I'm using a crutch," or "Taking medicine demonstrates a lack of faith." Yet these same people will have no qualms about using decongestants or pain relievers or other common medicines. Be thankful that chemists and biologists can understand the workings of the body to the extent that they can create medicines to intervene successfully in bodily malfunctions. Use medicines conservatively and according to careful medical supervision, but be open to their helpfulness.

In addition to a possible medical intervention, depression is usually treated with a psychotherapeutic approach, the use of insight and awareness that will prompt key adjustments in emotional and relationship management. Thought patterns, current and historical, will be analyzed, as will appropriate ways of handling common stresses and disappointments. As you identify adjustments that can be made in these areas you should be able to reverse patterns that helped cause the depression in the first place. Then you can prevent it from recurring in the future.

In the following chapters we will help you focus on many of the psychological contributors to depression, and we will help you discover ways to put in place coping skills for the purpose of producing more even and consistent emotions.

Rather than being threatened by your depression, use it as a springboard for growth. No one enjoys the pain and struggle it produces, yet most of us come to a real understanding of ourselves only when we have brushes with negative consequences.

2

Anger Turned Inward

Step 2. Know that anger can be uncovered and choices can be made regarding its purpose.

Depression is anger turned inward. When we address people regarding depression, this is one of the most common awarenesses that we discuss. Some depressed people are not at all surprised to hear such a statement. "I've had lots of anger issues for years," some will admit, "but I just never discovered what to do about them." Others who have a restricted understanding of their emotions will protest by saying, "I've never been the kind of person to fly into a rage, so I'm not sure your statement applies in my case."

One such person was Chuck. Mild-mannered and soft-spoken, he worked with a computer software company developing new products. Though he had trained for the ministry in his early twenties he had concluded he was not cut out for the work because of his shyness and awkwardness with people. Working with computers and calculations was more his style. He could go at his own pace without worrying about managing people problems.

Now in his late thirties, Chuck consulted Dr. Minirth because of an increasing dread of work and all other contact with the public. He had withdrawn from the few friends he had and was finding even the simple chores at home to be a burden. He was the father of four children ranging from six to thirteen, so his house was constantly a beehive of activity. But in recent months he had sidestepped as many family activities as his wife, Glenna, would allow. "I just want to be left alone" was his most common assertion.

Dr. Minirth recognized right away the telltale signs of major depression: several months of very poor sleep patterns, a significant loss of weight, increasing difficulty in becoming motivated for work, poor concentration, mental dullness. After thoroughly discussing with Chuck the symptoms bringing him to the clinic, Dr. Minirth suggested they begin a medical treatment of the problem. But he then explained, "My goal is for you to enjoy a life of stability without the use of medicines. Right now we'll use the medical approach as long as it is needed, but I want you to commit to learning about your emotional habits so you will not keep subjecting your personality to stressors that will perpetuate your problems with depression." That made sense to Chuck, so on Dr. Minirth's advice, he and Dr. Carter began a series of counseling sessions to help him understand his emotional patterns.

As Chuck described his lifestyle patterns, Dr. Carter noticed how often he referred to his frustrations and disappointments with people. Ever since his first child was born, Chuck had sensed that Glenna seemed less interested in him. She was so consumed with her role as mother that she had almost no time to be a wife. This left him feeling disappointed and used, but he reasoned it would do no good to mention his feelings because she wasn't going to change any time soon. Additionally, he had been feeling increasingly disgruntled at work. Never one to play up to his superiors, he felt he had been passed over for promotions because he was the unassuming kind of employee who was easily taken for granted.

Life with his extended family was also dissatisfactory. His father had died during his youth, and his mother was an ever-present influence in his life. She expected him to help her with odd jobs reserved for a man, and she reasoned that it was Chuck's duty to do them since she had never remarried. If he balked at a request she would readily use guilt to motivate him, knowing he would eventually capitulate. This displeased Glenna greatly, so when he would respond to his mother's many demands, she would become openly agitated. Chuck felt emotionally paralyzed because he could never figure out how to please both women. He chronically felt that life was a juggling act in which he had to keep the balls from crashing.

Can you see how Chuck had reasons for anger? Feeling neglected in his marriage, overwhelmed by the needs of four kids, used at work, dominated by his mother, he wanted to shout in despair: "Enough!" But he knew no one would adequately adjust to suit his needs no matter how loud he protested.

How about you? Have you ever felt that inward surge of tension, only to feel that expressing your feelings would be futile because others would probably not care about your needs? What are some fairly recent examples? (For instance, "My spouse never seems to be interested in my needs no matter how nicely I state them," or "My extended family would only criticize me if I revealed problems.")

1. _____

_____

2. _____

_____

3. _____
   _____

When your tensions mount inwardly like this, the emotion at the base of it all is anger, your emotion most closely linked to your desire for self-preservation. Many people fail to call anger by its name because they have a narrow, stereotypical picture of what anger is. "If I'm not yelling or openly complaining," they contend, "then I'm not really angry." They will admit to feelings of frustration or hurt or impatience, but that's different—or is it really?

For anger to be anger, you do not have to have a volcanic temper. It can be displayed in a wide array of behaviors and attitudes.

Look over the following list of traits and check the ones that could potentially apply to you:

__ Feeling irritated because of someone's imperfections or insensitivities.

__ Sulking when I realize others don't agree with my views or preferences.

__ Remaining frustrated because of the unfair circumstances I encounter.

__ Thinking critical thoughts about people's quirks.

__ Fretting about the minor details involved in my daily tasks.

__ Choosing to procrastinate on those jobs I dislike.

__ Speaking words of complaint behind a person's back.

__ Promising to do a favor, then resenting the fact that I have too much to do.

__ Avoiding people I probably need to confront.

__ Struggling with impatience.

__ Speaking in sharp tones.

__ Withdrawing from people, even when I know I probably shouldn't.

__ Feeling hurt when a person fails to recognize my needs or perceptions.

— Being disillusioned as I witness the repeated imperfections of people I want to admire.
— Holding resentments regarding others' insensitivities toward me.

Can you see how multidimensional anger can be? Yes, a shouting or openly disruptive person is angry, but that is not the only way anger can be expressed. When you catch yourself in one of the above behaviors, particularly if you behave this way repeatedly, you can be assured that anger is alive within your personality.

List three or four of the most common ways your anger is on display.

1. _____
2. _____
3. _____
4. _____

Don't be alarmed to discover that anger is a common visitor to your emotional system. No one is immune to it. We each encounter frustrations every day that arouse this response. Your goal is not to eliminate anger but to identify it and learn to make choices that will keep it from becoming any more harmful than it needs to be.

Dr. Carter remarked to Chuck, "As I listen to you describing your circumstances, I'm struck by the amount of frustrations that has piled up within you through the years. It seems that you have made a conscious decision to put a lid on your emotions, but in doing so, you've enabled those emotions to build a negative momentum that eventually takes its toll on you."

"I know I've got my share of agitations," Chuck said in mild pro-test, "but it's not going to do any good to say anything about my problems because I honestly believe people don't really care about what bothers me."

"Maybe you've trained them to think that way toward you." That statement startled Chuck as he considered for the first time that perhaps he was less a victim of circumstances than a victim of his own choices. The doctor's words carried a clear implication. *You can choose how you manage your emotions.* As simple as that thought seemed, Chuck realized it would have profound implications if he could learn to choose to manage his emotions differently than he had in the past.

"Sure enough, we need to be cautious in our methods of expressing anger," said Dr. Carter, "but let's understand that this emotion can have a legitimate function." Again, this thought was novel to Chuck. Legitimate? Anger? He had been so programmed to assume that it is always bad to be angry that he could hardly conceive of its legitimacy.

"Notice when you *don't* feel angry," Dr. Carter said. "You're not angry when people are kind or pleasant or cooperative. In those moments your emotions remain calm. Your anger is aroused, though, when others are rude or uncaring or insensitive. When you sense those things, your emotions are awakened. You don't like being treated disrespectfully so you feel the urge to take a stand of self-preservation for your worth, your needs, your convictions. Anger can propel you to hold firmly to the things you know are right and good."

"That makes sense," he replied, "because I *do* notice how I often wish people could treat me better. I'm *very* tired of feeling like my needs are being passed over while everyone else pushes their agenda on me."

"The problem you've had with anger lies in your reluctance to speak to the issues. Somehow you've become convinced that it will do no good to address your self-preservation needs, so you hold your feelings inside where they eventually develop a powerful self-destructive momentum. Depression becomes a virtual certainty at that point."

"But if I start expressing my anger, won't it appear selfish?" Chuck was expressing the misassumption that many depressed people make, that anger and selfishness are synonymous.

"It *could* be expressed in a harmful manner," replied Dr. Carter, "though you can take steps to keep that from being the case. You'll need to map out a plan to ensure your anger will be constructive rather than destructive."

As you consider your need to adjust your anger management, what hesitancies do you cling to that might hinder you from being open with this emotion? (For instance, "My mother used to lecture me that I'd better not show my temper," or "It probably won't change matters anyway if I tell people how I really feel.")

_____

_____

_____

Unhealthy Anger Choices

Though you can never be certain how others will respond to your expressions of anger, you can commit to having an appropriate manner of handling this emotion. To do so you will need to be aware that you handle your anger the way you do because of choices, and you can learn to choose the healthy options over the unhealthy. If you have experienced depression for any length of time you will recognize that your anger choices probably have favored one or more of three unhealthy choices: suppression, passive aggression, or open aggression. You will need to familiarize yourself instead with better choices: setting boundaries, speaking assertively, and forgiving.

Suppression

As Chuck and Dr. Carter continued their discussions, they explored Chuck's lifelong history of holding in his emotions in the valiant but futile attempt to appear unruffled. "Neither of my parents was skilled at handling emotions out in the open," he explained. "That doesn't mean we didn't experience emotions in our house, we just wouldn't resolve them clearly. My dad was the type who could blow up quickly, then be over it quickly. He had a hair-trigger temper, and you never knew exactly what might set him off."

"So the anger was expressed so rapidly and seemingly out of nowhere that you didn't have a chance to discuss it?"

"Exactly. When my dad got ticked off, my brothers and I knew better than to say anything back. It would produce nothing but grief if we did, so we learned to keep quiet." Then, shifting gears, he said, "Now Mother was a different story. She was the ultimate peacemaker who'd do anything to avoid a fuss. Many times she told me, 'It will do no good to complain because you'll only hear others complain in return.' She instilled in me the notion that I would have a much easier time in life if I just rode out my conflicts with the least resistance."

"You've learned that lesson well," said the doctor. "My impression is that your adult years have been spent perfecting the art of avoiding trouble, only you've been paying a high price with depression."

Years ago a local auto mechanic ran commercials on television imploring the public to hurry into one of his auto repair shops for regular engine tune-ups. His pitch centered on the fact that he could prevent many problems in the future if you would only bring your car in for inspection today. Then he'd sign off: "See me now or see me later!" Little did this auto repair pitchman know that he was also explaining a psychological principle.

When you choose to store your anger, reasoning that it would be futile to inform others of your needs and feelings, the anger does not just dissolve. It lingers weeks, months, years, even decades. A very high percentage of our depressed patients can look upon a past of holding anger in the false hope that it would one day just dissolve. But that day never comes. Instead, the individual becomes increasingly committed to a life of pretense, falsely portraying on the outside a calm that does not exist on the inside.

When the depression becomes so strong that it significantly disrupts that person's quality of life, we usually know that this individual has tried so hard for so long to avoid conflict that he has difficulty admitting even to himself how angry he really has felt.

How many of the following statements apply to you?

__ I hate conflict and often go out of my way to stay out of arguments and debates.

__ Too often I smile when I really feel frustration and annoyance building within.

__ Sometimes I do what others want me to do without explaining to them the hardship it creates.

__ I'm more worried about others' opinions than I really need to be.

__ I have decided that the best way to eliminate problems is to avoid certain people.

__ I have rehearsed strong "speeches" in private only to soften them significantly when it comes time to confront.

__ Few people would know by looking at me how frustrated I am with life.

__ I have thought frequently that nobody really knows or cares about the real me.

__ Even when people ask me for direct opinions I will still give the safe response.

__ I don't talk openly with others about the real extent of my hurt and pain.

How did you do? If you responded to five or more of these statements you probably have a long-standing history of suppressing your anger that can explain your inclination toward depression. Recognize that this pattern *is* an option, though not a good one. You choose suppression because you have reasoned that it is better than doing something else. In order to move away from this nonproductive option you will need to be convinced that the price to pay for it is too high.

What fallout have you experienced as a result of your ongoing suppression of anger? (For instance, "My frustration with my parents is so strong I can hardly talk with them now without becoming critical or cynical.")

_____

_____

_____

Dr. Carter explained to Chuck, "Your depression exists for a reason. When you told me that your family history did not encourage open exploration of emotions, I realized that you could be headed for real problems. We live in an imperfect world, meaning it is only normal to discuss our differences with one another. But when conflicts go months unresolved those imperfections seem larger than life. You feel overwhelmed by them because the sheer number of your unsolved problems continues to grow."

"I've always hated having to discuss conflicts because it only seems to produce *more* conflicts," Chuck said. "I'm not sure how I could change at this point in my life."

Wanting Chuck to see that the anger *would* surface if he continued suppressing it, Dr. Carter said, "Don't think suppressed anger just dies out. Usually it has a habit of showing up in passive-aggressive behaviors."

Passive Aggression

"I've heard the term *passive-aggressive*, but I'm not real sure what it is."

"Think first of the word *aggression*. This term implies that you are wanting to seek revenge against someone. You may have legitimate needs and feelings that have been overlooked so now you nurse a desire to register your irritation in some open way. But, true to your suppression habits, you don't want to be too open or vulnerable in your expressions. This is where the term *passive* comes in."

"You mean I act unbecomingly toward people in a more quiet way?"

"That's right. You still won't scream or slam doors, but you communicate some clear dissatisfaction. What do you think, Chuck? Is this something you can relate to?"

The sly smile that crossed his face told Dr. Carter they were right on target. "I guess I might be inclined to show my displeasures in subdued ways," he understated. "At least, Glenna tells me she has no problem knowing when I'm irritated."

Being an energized emotion, anger cannot remain stymied forever. It is going to be communicated in *some* form. In fact, depression itself can be a form of passive aggression. Through withdrawal, the depressed person is stating to his world, "Look, I'm tired of having to deal with pain and frustration so I'm taking a break, and I don't really care if you like it or not. I'm worn out!" Invariably, numerous passive-aggressive behaviors accompany depression.

Passive-aggressive anger is defined as preserving self's needs and convictions in a subdued manner. It is communicated without great regard for the feelings of the other persons involved. Likewise it usually involves some form of pretense or deception. For instance, a passive-aggressive person may spend an entire evening speaking to no one in the family. When asked if he is perturbed about anything, he may readily respond, "Why no, what would make you think anything's wrong?" This behavior seeks control with the least amount of vulnerability.

To determine if you ever manage your anger with passive aggression, check the following items that apply to you.

__ I have a history of procrastinating with my various projects.

__ Sometimes I'll promise to do someone a favor knowing I won't do it.

__ I have had a problem with tardiness.

__ When I become irritated I may go for hours without speaking to the person I'm in conflict with.

__ I have asked people to help me with my problems, then failed to follow through with their helpful suggestions.

__ When I am in the midst of a disagreement, a major priority is to end the conversation as quickly as possible.

__ I become annoyed when people try to force me to live outside my normal daily routine.

__ I may do what I am required to do, but you might not get my best effort.

__ I may talk openly about relationship problems behind someone's back but will not take the opportunity to openly discuss the problems with that person.

__ After making a commitment, I may begin thinking about how I could renegotiate or get out of it.

If you checked five or more of the above responses, you probably have established a pattern of letting your anger be expressed in this quietly manipulative manner. Temporarily you may feel a type of satisfaction, knowing that you are quietly controlling those who would thwart you. But in the long run you are shooting yourself in the foot because the anger is not successfully resolved. Passive-aggressive anger just lingers and lingers, eventually imprisoning the person in sour, frustrated moods.

As Chuck and Dr. Carter discussed this method of anger management, Chuck nodded and confessed, "This is me to a tee. I've never liked confrontation, and I'll go out of my way to avoid arguments. But I have a hard time making my frustrations just dissolve."

"What is your earliest recollection regarding this passive style of expressing anger?"

"Oh, it's been going on as long as I can remember. My father was always a very dominant factor in my life . . . you know, very opinionated, always making suggestions. There wasn't much room for variance with him. Mom tried to be easygoing, and she'd never stand up to him. Her philosophy was 'peace at any cost.' I guess you could say I learned from her to go underground with my feelings."

"So just because irritabilities weren't openly displayed, we can't assume that it was always harmonious in your home. Agitating feelings were communicated without being accompanied by shouting."

Chuck nodded, then continued to discuss with Dr. Carter how he had carried this pattern into his relationship with his wife, Glenna. He felt perpetually frustrated in their inability to discuss calmly how they felt about their differences, so he resorted to many quiet ways to register his frustrations. For instance, when their children were young he would appear busy with "important" projects when he knew she needed assistance. Or he would openly agree with her opinions about family discipline, then proceed to do whatever he wanted, despite their agreements.

Have you ever managed anger this way? What was present in your early family history that encouraged you to express your anger in quiet manipulations? (For instance, "My mother was very opinionated so I learned to outwardly comply; then when she wasn't looking, I'd be defiant.")

_____

_____

_____

What conditions exist in your current circumstances that perpetuate passive expressions of anger? (For instance, "My work environment is very regimented; there is no room for differentness or uniqueness.")

_____

_____

_____

How does your passive style of anger management increase your inclination toward depression? (For instance, "I know my actions frustrate others, and as a result we are less inclined to work out our differences.")

_____

_____

_____

The most seductive element of passive-aggressive anger is the temporary sense of power it gives the user. Most depressed people have a history of feeling dominated or overlooked, so they relish the taste of dominance that can be theirs, even though it may be short-lived. In order to break the cycle of depression arising from passive aggression, these people will need to acknowledge that inner satisfaction is not permanently anchored in dominance or control but in inner freedom exercised separate from competitive relating.

Too often, though, people will assume that they should take a "no-holds-barred" approach to anger, meaning they can go to the other extreme of becoming openly aggressive with anger.

Open Aggression

When most people think of anger it is this category that comes to mind—shouting, criticism, blaming, accusing, being overwhelming. Many people who have a history of hidden or subdued anger will eventually explode with vile eruptions as they realize they cannot keep up the walls required for passive anger or suppressed anger. It is not at all uncommon for us to hear stories, usually told sheepishly, about depressed people who went into wild tirades of cursing or screaming. The lid has been held on their emotions too long, and the anger can no longer be contained.

Another common pattern we see is less dramatic but equally debilitating. The depressed person can become persistently grouchy and edgy. No longer willing to keep the anger quiet, regular verbal jabs are slung about as pessimism, criticism, and futility are openly registered. This, too, is considered aggressive anger.

For instance, the last straw that prompted Chuck to seek the initial appointment with Dr. Minirth involved a volatile scene at home with Glenna. He had spent a Saturday morning running errands that he didn't want to run for his mother. He came home wanting to do nothing but relax for a couple of hours. So when his wife reminded him that he needed to tend to an unfinished project with their son, Chuck exploded. "What am I, some sort of slave? Do I just exist to satisfy everyone else? Don't my needs ever matter?" He spent the next thirty minutes saying hateful things to her, venting many resentments that had been stored inside for months.

As you might imagine, the next several days at Chuck's house were miserable, a very uncomfortable standoff. When Chuck realized his tirade only widened the gap between himself and his wife, his depressed feelings hit him full force. He found no motivation to work or even to engage in routine activities. He accused Glenna of being a user who cared little about him as a person. He could barely eat or sleep.

When Dr. Carter asked if this experience had ever occurred before, he responded, "Every six months or so I become very tense and I feel like I could burst. This last outburst was one of my worst, but it's not the only time I've done it." He admitted that in the two or so weeks prior to the outburst he had been unusually cranky and impatient. "It's like I was just waiting for an excuse to let off steam."

Has this ever happened to you? What events have occurred in the recent or distant past that resulted in open expressions of aggression? (For instance, "Two Christmases ago I made a spectacle of telling my brother how strongly I disliked his treatment of me.")

1. _____

_____

2. _____

_____

3. _____

_____

To get an idea of your potential for openly aggressive anger, check the following items that could apply to you:

__ Sometimes I find myself verbalizing too much cynicism or pessimism.

__ I have been openly rude or rejecting toward someone lately.

__ There was a time recently when I had a good point to make in a confrontation, but I stated it so strongly that it did not accomplish the desired result.

__ At times I struggle with being critical.

__ Lately, I've been fed up with people's insensitivity, and it shows in my attitude and behavior.

__ My impatient feelings are exhibited more strongly than I would like.

__ I have been unloading my frustrations on people in subordinate positions (children, store clerks, employees, etc.).

__ If someone says something confrontational to me, I'm likely to snap right back at that person.

— I'm growing increasingly weary with life and don't really care who knows it.

— It's harder lately to be the friendly person I used to be.

If you responded to five or more of these items, it is likely that you are not succeeding in masking your anger with diplomacy or learning constructive ways to communicate it. At the very best, you can say your anger is not being stored in a suppressive style where it will quietly turn sour. But neither is it being released in a manner that will free you from its ill effects. Because aggressive behavior rarely solves any problems, the anger will continue to recycle, ensuring ongoing inclinations toward bitterness, resentment, and, yes, depression.

Anger managed in this openly destructive manner only increases your feelings of shame and inadequacy, ingredients that perpetuate your tendencies toward depression. Though you are not making the mistake of bottling your emotions, you *are* mistakenly elevating yourself at another's expense to the extent that you are creating more problems than you are able to solve. This then backfires, causing you to feel overwhelmed with your problems.

When you realize you have poorly communicated your anger, what self-blaming statements are you likely to think? (For instance, "Now I know no one will take me seriously again.")

_____

_____

_____

Why do you let your anger out in abrasive patterns? (For instance, "For years, I've assumed that no one will listen if I just speak in a normal tone of voice.")

_____

_____

_____

33

Depression and Choice

As you identify the patterns of anger being described, you may notice an implied theme in our discussion: You are not obliged to manage your anger in disruptive patterns. You have a choice. If you want, you can suppress your anger or be passive with it or be openly abrasive. It's your decision. Most people who become depressed will admit to choosing one or all three of these patterns of anger, and as they become aware of the painfulness of the consequences they may decide that better options should be pursued. By understanding the place of choices you move one step closer to taking responsibility for your depression.

At this point, though, let's make something very clear. You do not necessarily have to take responsibility for the circumstances that produced the anger. In many instances you had no choice regarding the events that so negatively affected your emotions. Your responsibility is not for the inappropriate behavior of others but for your ultimate reaction to it.

Think for a moment of some anger-producing possibilities that you may have had little choice over:

- Your spouse turns out to be an overbearing, insensitive critic who shows little ability genuinely to love.

- As a child you were sexually abused by an unstable relative.

- You were laid off from work because your company had to downsize.

- In the aftermath of a divorce, some friends rejected you because they did not make the effort to understand your perspectives.

- In spite of your efforts to provide a good life, your son or daughter has been very rebellious and unappreciative.

- Your mate died very unexpectedly and at an untimely period of life.

- Your superiors at work cannot appreciate the good qualities you bring to the company.

These circumstances, and many more, may be beyond the realm of your control. At the time you experienced them you may have had your hands tied, leaving you with an intense feeling of victimization.

Looking into the recent past as well as the distant past, what circumstances out of your control caused you to experience anger? (For instance, "I felt anger for years because my father was very overbearing.")

1. _____
2. _____
3. _____

It may seem odd to suggest that in these unwanted situations you had a choice regarding anger. Initially, you did not. The anger came upon you whether you wanted it or not. But at some point in your life we can assume that you *did* have choices regarding the power you allowed that anger to have in your life. If you choose, you can continue harboring the anger in one of the destructive patterns that perpetuate depression or you can decide that it is time to pursue better alternatives.

Can you see the hope that can arise from the understanding of the role of choices? This means you need not remain a victim to circumstance. It means you can draw upon an inner strength that has lain dormant. It means you can move on with a life guided by your notions of healthiness.

Choosing new patterns of anger will not be easy or natural because we tend to be creatures of habit. But it can be done! In the next chapter we will examine some of those better alternatives.

But before you move on, what commitment can you make to yourself regarding your future choices of anger management? (For instance, "I am aware that I can continue to choose silence when I feel frustrated, but I have decided that a more open communication of my feelings is in order.")

_____

_____

_____

_____

3

The Other Side of Anger

Step 3. Become committed to healthy boundaries and assertions.

Once depression-prone people understand that choices are involved in their management of emotions, they often ask: "Does this mean I have a right to be angry?" Let's be very careful in our answer to this. Too often when we think of rights we can be operating from a selfish frame of reference, thinking of what is best for me and me alone. So let's make an adjustment and rephrase the question. Exchange the word "right" with the word "responsibility." Do I have a responsibility to be angry? This considers what is best not just for me but for all persons involved.

Many times emotional expressions are irresponsible. As we have already seen, it can be harmful to oneself as well as to the people who are receiving expressions of anger.

In some instances, though, the communication of anger is an act of responsibility. Since anger is the emotional push to preserve personal needs and convictions, there are times when it has its place in healthy relationships. No relationship will ever unfold without glitches. Some pitfalls will occur, as will mistakes and insecurities. Certainly in those moments there is a need for open communication regarding personal needs. Furthermore, blatant wrongs may have occurred, and it would be irresponsible to let those wrongs pass without openly addressing them.

Depressed persons usually need to retrain their minds to acknowledge that anger can at times be a legitimate emotion that should be openly expressed. Part of the healing arises from taking the lid off inner tensions and attempting to be proactive in letting others know their hurts, their needs, their convictions—that is, heading off future problems by letting others know ahead of time how they feel in particular situations and communicating so as to prevent conflicts before they arise. The key lies in the delivery.

> Can you think of three or four areas in your life in which you need to be more proactive in addressing your feelings of anger? (For instance, "I need to give in less often when my kids make untimely demands," or "I need to remove myself from extended family members who have been unapologetically abusive toward me.")
>
> 1. _____
> 2. _____
> 3. _____
> 4. _____

As Dr. Carter gave him permission to disclose the extent of his angry feelings, Chuck admitted, "I've felt for years like people have been walking on my feelings. It's like I've got tire marks all along my front because I've allowed myself to be run over so many times. I can be good-natured, but I've learned the hard way that there are many people who are very willing to take advantage of my style."

Nodding slowly Dr. Carter reflected, "It will feel unnatural to develop a much firmer nature, but in certain instances that's what you'll need." Then to allay Chuck's discomfort with that idea he added, "This doesn't imply you'll have to go to the other extreme of being as tough as nails, because that's never going to be your style. But it does mean you'll need to do a better job of drawing lines of self-preservation."

To keep anger from festering and becoming foundational for depression, Dr. Carter explained that there would be three areas in which Chuck could make personal adjustments: boundaries, assertiveness, and forgiveness.

Chuck could not stop all disruptive events from occurring. He could not force people to respect him. He could not make others consider his needs. But he *could* learn to respond more decisively to clear incidences of wrong or insensitivity. He *could* become a better advocate for his legitimate feelings and beliefs. He *could* be more openly self-respecting. In making these adjustments, his struggles with depression would not necessarily be permanently erased, but they could be eased substantially.

Dr. Carter explained, "Before we examine the actual changes you could make, you'll need earnestly to desire to be different. Your changes won't always feel natural. What about it? Are you up to it?"

"Well, I'm not sure what you've got in mind, but I know *something's* got to change," Chuck said. "My history has been one of extremes; I'm either too harsh with my emotions or too suppressive."

"In treating your depression we will need to clean out your emotional garbage, but we'll want to do so in a way that's constructive, not destructive. New insights can go a long way in giving you hope."

Boundaries

A major problem encountered by depressed people is boundaries that are not respected. In healthy relationships it is reasonable to assume that no two people can feel or think or act the same. You are you; I am me. We are separate. We are different, and that's not just okay, it's a cause to celebrate. Thriving relationships, then, will openly encourage uniqueness. They will allow variance in perceptions. They will acknowledge differing needs and preferences. In short, boundaries are respected. Sameness is not required. Individual tastes are allowed.

What do you believe about boundaries? When is it good to let differentness be shown in your relationships? (For instance, "I don't always crave the same social activities as my spouse, but that's okay," or "As long as I get my work done on the job, it can be reasonable for me to approach my tasks differently than a coworker.")

_____

_____

_____

People with a history of depression often tell us, "I've never felt comfortable in revealing the things about me that might not coincide with the preferences of others." In fact, many have deeply learned that it is painful or harmful to be open about personal uniqueness, so they carry their feelings inwardly with no one really knowing what lies within. No wonder bitterness and futility build to a boiling point!

Check the following statements that potentially would apply to you:
__ When someone expresses strong opinions, I am inclined to keep my opinions to myself.
__ I feel that I'm constantly asked to do for others, but rarely does anyone care about my feelings or needs.
__ Most people would be surprised to learn just how upset I feel much of the time.

__ I have experienced hurts that I have told virtually no one about.

__ When I was younger I rarely felt free to expose the full extent of my needs.

__ When I express a weakness or hurt, it is often met with someone telling me what to do to remedy it.

__ I often assume that my perceptions are not as valuable as those of others.

__ My problem is that I too willingly defer to others' agendas.

If you responded to four or more of these items, you probably have a history of feeling that your boundaries are not respected. More firmness will be needed as you show others you are not always going to be the way they insist you should be.

"Theoretically, I can accept what you're telling me," said Chuck, "but practically, I'm not sure I'm up to the task. I mean, my mother is a pretty demanding woman, yet she's also sweet and I love her. It would blow her away if she knew the extent of the resentments that I have. I'd hate to hurt her."

"So you've decided that the best way to handle your increasingly sour mood is to hold in your feelings." Dr. Carter paused a moment to let Chuck reflect. Then he added, "Surely she senses a gap in your relationship, and even if she's oblivious, I'm hearing that your love for her is diminishing. In the short run it may feel awkward to establish boundaries, but I'm assuming you will have a much cleaner relationship with her when you do."

Setting boundaries means you will let what is distinctive about you be known. You will set stipulations when necessary. You will coach others regarding the ways they can more accurately respond to your needs.

For instance, let's go back through the statements you just responded to and look at the legitimate alternatives:

41

__ When someone expresses a strong opinion, I can still hold unwaveringly to my differing beliefs or perceptions.

__ As I am being constantly asked to do things by others, I have permission to say "no" or "not now."

__ Rather than holding in my feelings to give a false favorable impression, I can tell people how I feel so my emotions won't bitterly build inside me.

__ I can tell others about the things that hurt me, realizing I don't need to apologize for my feelings.

__ Though my youthful days were typified by hiding my needs, I can choose as an adult to be transparent.

__ When someone gives me unsolicited remedies for my feelings, I can explain that it's understanding, not advice, that I would really appreciate.

__ I can remind myself that my perceptions are just as valid as anyone else's.

__ Though I want to be known as cooperative, I can realize I'm not duty-bound to defer automatically to others' agendas.

Go back through the above statements and check the ones that express your desire to change in the days immediately ahead. Are you up to it? If others cannot figure out your boundaries perhaps you can do a better job of educating them. It will feel odd at first, but you can do it.

As an example, Chuck realized he had allowed depression to creep into his personality because he had rarely explained his needs and hurts to his wife, extended family, and fellow employees. On those rare occasions when he *had* done so, he would quickly back down when questioned, leaving him feeling even more exasperated than before.

Who do you need to establish better boundaries with? How will you accomplish this? (For instance, "I will give myself permission to speak as an adult with my father rather than letting him run my life as he tends to do.")

_____

_____
_____

_____

Assertiveness

Following close on the heels of boundaries is the practice of assertiveness, which can be defined as standing firmly for your needs and convictions while also being mindful of the needs of others. As you become committed to assertiveness, understand first what it is not. Assertiveness is not abrasiveness or being pushy or hardheaded, as some might assume. Assertiveness involves being forthright while simultaneously being considerate. It implies that you will be open and genuine about who you are. You believe strongly enough in the legitimacy of your needs that you will not let them sit unaddressed.

Dr. Minirth spoke with a woman, Patricia, about her lack of assertiveness and said, "As I've gotten to know you, I am impressed that you have a balanced understanding of the things you need from others. You want to be respected, yet I don't sense that you go so far that you are demanding or selfish."

Patricia had a hard time receiving compliments, so her face turned red as she responded, "I wish that I had the same confidence that you have in me. I'm always second-guessing myself."

She had come to the clinic because she was "completely burned out," as she put it. Her husband of twenty-five years was so insensitive to her needs that she long ago gave up on trying to get him to hear her. Besides, she rationalized to herself, she was accustomed to feeling neglected because she had little feeling of connectedness in her developmental years with her parents, especially her father. For most of her adulthood she had tried just to accept her emptiness, but now in her late forties she was weary of this plan. She wanted more from life.

In Dr. Minirth's first interview with her, she displayed the symptoms of depression that indicated she had given up. Poor social contacts, wanting to sleep at every opportunity, excessive weight gain from overeating, poor motivation and concentration in daily tasks, general pessimism. He noticed she was doing the bare minimum to keep her life in some semblance of order.

"I'm willing to help you in any way I can so you can overcome your depression," said Dr. Minirth, "but I also want to see that you are just as eager, if not more so, to take the steps needed to change your lifestyle."

Patricia felt like the girl who had her hand slapped because she was being asked to be more responsible, but then she realized the doctor was right. Indeed she had been on the receiving end of poor treatment, so it was only normal that she felt disgruntled. Yet, she also had to admit that she had caved in to her depressed feelings because she had specifically chosen not to take many stands of self-preservation. "I'm going to need your help," she said, "but I really do want to change."

The two discussed at length how she needed to reverse the trends of her personal history by being more direct with others about her needs. "There are numerous ways you can establish assertiveness and overcome your tendency toward depression," said Dr. Minirth. "For instance, how often do you wish for someone to do you a favor but instead of openly saying what you need you remain quiet and then feel hurt from others' inattentiveness?"

"That happens all the time, I guess. I'm afraid I don't speak up very often. I want others to figure it out on their own." Then she sighed deeply. "But it seems like they rarely do."

"Let's think of another possibility," Dr. Minirth continued. "How skilled are you at staking out your position in a dispute, then not backing down when someone tries to invalidate what you feel?"

"You got me again," she replied. "I feel like when I *do* finally get the nerve to say something it's probably going to be rebutted, and since I'm not a very good debater I usually can't think of a good comeback so I just keep quiet." Then another pause. "I'm beginning to see the point you're trying to make."

"By the way," said the doctor, "as you speak assertively, keep in mind that it is not your job to sell people regarding your needs, nor are you attempting to overpower anyone. Your job is to stand firmly on what you believe and to behave in accordance to your well-laid plans, realizing others may or may not agree with you at that precise moment.

"As you develop a reputation for assertiveness," he continued, "others can eventually learn that you are not just a dominating shrew who is trying to be overwhelming. Rather, you are showing yourself to be a calm but firm person who believes it is reasonable to stand for the things you know are right."

The required adjustments for people like Patricia and Chuck rarely come naturally. When you have had a habit of sitting on your feelings for long stretches of time, change feels odd. Yet to stay in the same old maladaptive habits of mishandling your emotions is to encourage ongoing depression. The price is too high *not* to change.

How about you? In what areas do you need to develop more successful assertiveness? (For instance, "My husband doesn't take me seriously when I ask him to eat dinner with the rest of the family; I need to quit preparing his dinner at nine o'clock.")

———————————————————————————————
———————————————————————————————
———————————————————————————————

Being assertive means you willingly take initiative in your life. You are not a reactor who waits for others to set the pace for you. Instead, you know who you are and what you believe, and you live according to your own directives. Both Patricia and Chuck had to rethink their habits in this respect. Both had convinced themselves that others were taking advantage of them, when in fact the deeper problem was lack of initiative.

Can you relate? In what ways do you need to react less and initiate more? (For instance, "Rather than always checking to determine if my spouse likes my preferences, I need to be decisive in planning my day.")

_____

_____

_____

Notice the following examples of assertiveness that you could commit to improve upon.

• Rather than altering your day's schedule for someone else's minor preferences, you can explain that you already have your activities planned.

• You will express your opinion firmly in a family dispute *without* having to justify it.

• You can talk to a friend or family member about long-standing needs that have been overlooked.

• When someone makes an unreasonable or untimely request, you can let that person know that you cannot do it.

• You can be more persistent in explaining how others can assist you with your overcrowded schedule.

Being assertive means that you recognize that it is legitimate to be human and to have preferences and needs. It means you are committed to pursuing relationships that are anchored in that realization.

Often adults fail to assert themselves properly because of long-standing patterns, going as far back as childhood. To reverse the trend, you will first need to become mindful that you are no longer a child who is obliged to capitulate under someone else's pressure. For instance, Chuck realized he was depressed in large part because he had assumed in childhood that he had no power to overcome his father's forcefulness or his mother's subtle guilt trips. Powerful emotions that had quietly built up within him were displayed as depression in his adult years. He had become habituated to self-put-downs and feebleness, traits that served him poorly.

Dr. Carter explained, "Chuck, as a boy you had no encouragement to act upon your own beliefs and initiatives. You learned it was safer to be a reactor. But now as an adult, it doesn't have to be that way. Perhaps now you can realize that your parents had their own problems they were playing out on you, but you are no longer under any obligation to keep their patterns alive within your personality. You *can* chart your own course."

"I like the sound of that," Chuck replied, "although I've got to admit that it's going to take some real adjustment for me to operate on these new assumptions."

"To switch from a depressive style to an initiating style will feel odd, no doubt," said Dr. Carter. "You'll need to be sure you're really ready to change." Noting the look of curiosity that statement created, he explained, "Some people say they want to be free from their depression, but when people like me encourage them to be more open and straightforward, they balk. We tend to remain with things that are familiar, even if they are distasteful, because it can be scary to move into new and uncharted territories."

Are you like Chuck in that respect? Have you known that you needed to take more initiative but have failed to do so because it felt too strange or different?

How would you have to adjust your thinking in order to develop more motivation to be assertive? (For instance, "I'd have to be convinced my needs are as legitimate as anyone else's," or "I'd need to learn to justify my preferences less.")

_____

_____

_____

Sometimes to break long-standing tendencies toward nonassertion you may find it helpful to talk with the people who were responsible for training you to hold in your feelings. For example, though it was very awkward for him, Chuck sat down with his mother and discussed with her that he could not respond any longer to her guilt trips as he had done so often in the past. Initially, she was defensive in her response, but Chuck had decided in advance that he would not be harsh or pushy in his mannerisms nor would he back down. In the weeks following, she called him less, but that then freed Chuck to keep in touch with her without feeling the same pressure to perform dutifully as he had in the past.

What assertions do you need to make with people who have been involved in your long-standing patterns of suppressed emotions? (For instance, "I need to explain to my father that I will no longer react fearfully to his powerful commands," or "I can explain to my adult son that I will no longer support him financially since he can do this for himself.")

_____

_____

_____

These confrontations may be quite difficult, particularly when the related anger is very painful and intense. For instance, Patricia admitted that she began holding in her feelings as a young girl because her father had been sexually abusive toward her. "It's impossible to explain how betrayed I have felt knowing my own father could be as selfish as he was. He's more mellow now, but I still feel deep resentment toward him that has never been expressed."

With Dr. Minirth's guidance, she composed a letter to her father telling him how hurt she was that she had been so mistreated as a girl. In it she explained her difficulties with self-confidence, with trust, with communicating needs. Her writing was not done with a caustic approach, but it was firm and to the point. Later she said, "When I wrote out my feelings, I felt a huge burden lifted from me. I realized I was no longer obligated to cover for him by denying the very real anger I felt. I had no idea of the release I would feel by being assertive regarding my feelings."

In her letter, Patricia outlined how she intended to handle family obligations differently, citing several pertinent examples. She explained that she did not require any adjustments from him but that she was going to be a different, more adult, communicator toward him. She then picked an appropriate time to read the things to him she had written, knowing he would take her more seriously if he heard it directly from her.

Perhaps your old wounds are not as deep as Patricia's, or maybe they are. Nonetheless, if you are experiencing depression you can probably cite some old wounds that finally need mending.

What methods do you need to use to lay some of your old tensions to rest? (For instance, "I need to have a long talk with my brother about the pain that has gone unresolved for years.")

How can you know that your efforts to address problems are indeed assertive, not aggressive? (For instance, "I'll keep my tone of voice from being judgmental," or "I'll refrain from character assassination.")

_____

_____
_____

_____

You can know most certainly that your efforts are true assertions by the lack of coercion in your voice. Being assertive means you are standing for truth without desiring dominance. You merely want to relate as one adult to another. Whether or not it creates change in others, you will notice that you feel less depressed and defeated when you stand firmly for legitimate needs and beliefs.

Forgiveness

Because no two people ever operate from the same agendas, assertiveness and boundary setting do not always produce the desired results. For example, suppose you are both calm and crystal clear in expressing a conviction to an inappropriate family member, yet he responds to you as if you are speaking in a foreign language. Or suppose you hold fast to an appropriate conviction to the extent that it causes a former close friend to snub you forevermore. What do you do?

Has this ever happened to you? Have you ever attempted to express a conviction or need only to realize that the other person considers your feelings so lightly that no adjustment will be forthcoming? It is at this point that many people crumble and fall back into their nonproductive emotional patterns. For instance, Chuck had told Dr. Carter that he had found Glenna resistant to productive communication early in their marriage, so he had decided just to live with his despair—the result being his ongoing depression.

What experiences of assertion have you had that have produced virtually nothing tangibly rewarding? (For instance, "My step-father has never made an effort to know my needs no matter how strongly I declare them.")

1. _____

_____

2. _____

_____

How has the resulting frustration over your failed assertiveness contributed to your depression? (For instance, "It's easy for me to assume I'm a nobody because my feelings are not taken very seriously.")

1. _____

_____

2. _____

_____

Though it is desirable that others would react favorably to your efforts to stand firmly for your needs and convictions, when they do not you are not relegated to poor emotional choices. You still have the option to forgive, which also assumes that you will accept reality for what it is. You can have a healthy emotional response even when the people around you are not operating from healthy choices.

The vast majority of depressed people we counsel are held captive to depressed emotions because they choose not to come to terms with circumstances that will never conform to their ideal expectations. Not that their hopes are wrong. . . . Is it wrong to wish a father had not abused his daughter? Or to wish a spouse would put the marriage in its proper place of priority? Or to hope that friends would accept one's feelings without an air of judgment? No! Most

51

depressed people stay depressed not because their convictions are wrong but because they choose to fume over problems that cannot be resolved in neatly arranged packages.

Pessimistic reality causes us to conclude that not all problems can be successfully resolved in a pleasing or fair manner. Others can keep problems from being resolved because they are stubborn, or unrepentant, or in denial, or arrogant, or noninsightful, or fearful of change. Though your eagerness tells you that change could happen *if only others* would heed your legitimate assertions, you can go out of bounds emotionally if you make no room for others' unbending responses. This is where the need for forgiveness comes in.

Before we define this, pause for a moment: What do you think about forgiveness? Is it a worthy trait? Do you feel compromised when you forgive? Does it offer too easy a way out for offenders? What struggles do you have with forgiveness? (For instance, "If I forgive my ex-husband after all the mistreatment he gave me I'd feel like he got away with his own selfish agenda.")

_____

_____

_____

_____

To ready yourself for forgiveness, let go of the scorecard. Drop your insistence for fairness. Set aside your picture of the ideal world. Make room for ugly truth. We do not imply that you no longer should stand on any conviction. Nor are we suggesting that your hurt is out of line. But we are saying that some things are out of your control. Let them be in God's hands. To forgive means that you will relinquish your legitimate reasons to feel angry and hurt, and you will shift your focus away from others' inappropriateness and toward your own positive growth goals. Though you do not condone wrong, you realize it will happen.

Forgiveness is not synonymous with the suppression of anger, which is a phony portrayal that all is well when in reality it is not. Rather, forgiveness is a recognition of your own human limits. It is your realization that you are not going to right all wrongs because you are not God.

Think about the origins of your depression. Who has frustrated you? Who has let you down or treated you unfairly? Openly acknowledge that you are normal in your feelings of hurt or betrayal. Then ask: Have I done all I can to constructively establish my boundaries? My uniqueness? Have I been willing to speak out when necessary? Am I committed to honest communication about my feelings—even if the other person is not?

Then question: Can I choose to live without bitterness and defeat even if that other person fails to respect my convictions? Though I don't like unresolved conflicts, can I pursue my goals for healthy living in spite of the lack of cooperation from others?

Breaking free from the grip of depression will not be easy because it will require you not only to act differently but to *think* differently.

What new thoughts will you have to hold to aid your forgiveness process? (For instance, "I've decided it's not worth my time to live in reaction to my father's stubborn ways," or "I can forgive because I'd prefer not to live with the defeat caused by depression.")

_____

_____

_____

A breakthrough came for Patricia as she and Dr. Minirth discussed that she could get out from under her cloud of depression in part by forgiving her father for the wrongs he had committed. The doctor explained, "I don't want to suggest in any way that we will lightly overlook your father's past abuse, but I hope that you can conclude that his opinions or his perceptions no longer have to shape your direction in life. You can be free from his rejection by accepting the reality that he was a troubled man who did not give you what was rightfully due."

"I'd like that very much," she replied tearfully. "I've held on to my memories because I've wanted so many questions answered and so many wrongs corrected. But I'm at a point now where I can live without having everything tied down. I've got more to live for than just to worry about his problems."

> What about you? What benefit could be found as you choose to forgive wrongs done toward you? (For instance, "I'd have more energy to pursue relationships that could be rewarding.")

1. _____
2. _____
3. _____

A mistake people often make when struggling with depression is that they try solely to correct problems externally (for instance, trying to get others to be more accepting or accommodating). We encourage you to pursue the internal adjustments as well, such as choosing forgiveness. In doing so, you are not as readily thwarted by the unchanging or unaware qualities of others, but you are more of the initiator for your own personal stability.

4

Inadequacy Feelings Settle In

Step 4. Believe in yourself. Know your worth and value as a person.

Predictably, people overcome by depression report losing their zeal for living. No longer optimistic, they allow pessimistic thoughts to dominate. They assume failure even before it happens. Painful experience has caused them to assume that others no longer have faith in them, but more pointedly the depressed people have lost faith in themselves.

Repeatedly when we counsel depressed people we hear phrases like: "I don't know" or "I'm not sure" or "I just can't." These phrases reveal that they have accepted a failed view of self. Their failures and disappointments prompt them to concede that they do not have the necessary strength required to contend with the strains that await them.

Usually their feelings of inadequacy are the direct result of very real disappointments:

- Plans they had once felt optimistic about have ended in failure.

- Family relationships have brought colossal feelings of discouragement.

- People they thought highly of have rejected them.

- They feel overburdened by persistent financial strains.

- Their ability to keep up with career expectations has not been up to desired capacities.

- Life has been more of a struggle than it should be.

- They realize their mistakes have genuinely hurt people who once trusted them explicitly.

- Compared to others, they seem to have more failures, fewer successes.

- It becomes clear that their performance aspirations were idealistic illusions.

A creeping feeling of personal inadequacy overcomes depressed people as they assume their goals to connect or to impress or to achieve are no longer attainable. We usually hear these people exclaim, "No amount of effort or adjustment is going to make my problems go away." They then falsely assume that they can no longer be reasonably content because they don't have what it takes to make good things happen.

In her initial interview with Dr. Minirth, Suzette described herself in strongly negative terms. "I can't afford to be optimistic anymore.

I've had too many problems in the past to assume that life will be any different in the future." Currently single and in her mid-thirties, Suzette described her life as one overall disappointment. "I got married soon after I finished college," she explained, "but it only lasted four years. My ex was not a very highly motivated person, which is a nice way of saying he was very lazy. And after repeatedly pleading to get him to hold down steady work I just left him. Once I was gone from the house I never spoke to him again. Still haven't.

"I thought that would relieve me of my frustrations at the time, but now it seems that was only the beginning for a whole new set of problems. I've made a lot of poor choices since then, and right now I'm so down on myself that I just don't see a way out." She explained how she had become involved in both alcohol abuse and promiscuity. She had attempted to get with a cleaner crowd by going to church, but she found herself acting no differently with the church folks than with anyone else.

"I've worn out my welcome with my friends because I've been so moody they don't know which me they'll encounter whenever they call. So now they don't call. And I've gotten to where I don't care. I'm spending a lot of my free time by myself, and, though it's not very fulfilling, at least I don't make as many mistakes as I could otherwise." Her face showed great dejection, and she spoke in flat, weary tones.

Dr. Minirth asked, "Did you ever struggle with these feelings prior to the divorce?"

Nodding slowly, Suzette replied, "Off and on. I've never felt like I was quite up to speed with the rest of the crowd. Even as far back as grade school I remember wishing I could be friends with certain popular kids, and this problem continued in my teen years. I was involved in many activities, don't get me wrong. But I always felt I was one or two steps away from the inner circle. It's worse now than before, but this is definitely a trend for me.

"Going through a failed marriage only made my problem worse. I guess in your early years you at least have the hope that one day things will be better. But now that I'm all grown up, I'm finding that 'one day' hasn't come yet. I get real down on myself because I just can't seem to turn my problems around."

Have you ever felt this way? To what extent is your depression fed by feelings of inadequacy?

To get an idea of the extent of this problem, check the following statements that apply to you:

__ I often feel overwhelmed by the tasks I have to perform each day.

__ When I'm interacting with others I try to put my best foot forward, but I'm not sure I'm "pulling it off."

__ Before starting a task I can feel so uncertain that I don't even put out a good effort.

__ I frequently worry about how other people perceive me.

__ Even when people compliment me I wonder if they would still do so if they knew the real me.

__ I envy other people who seem to have it all together. I wish I could be that way.

__ It's easier to stay away from social contacts; that way I won't set myself up for disappointments.

__ My life has taken more wrong turns than I once had assumed would happen.

__ There is something about my personality that seems to self-destruct or fall short.

__ I doubt that I have positive traits to offer others.

Each of us struggles with feelings of uncertainty sometimes, so don't be alarmed to realize this is happening to you. If you checked five or more of these statements, though, you are likely to feel inadequate more than most. Your pessimism regarding self can be a major contributor to depression.

What negative thoughts about self seem to be most recurrent in your mind? (For instance, "Once people get to know me they'll probably grow tired of me.")

_____

_____

_____

As we examine how your feelings of inadequacy are linked to your depression, let's underscore two major thoughts:

1. There are clearly defined reasons that explain the presence of this problem; and
2. With awareness and the proper motivation you can reverse your inclination toward your pessimistic self-evaluation.

Developing Personal Competence

When you were a child were you capable of managing your emotions in a reasonable fashion? Yes and no. We say no because children are often untamed in their emotional expressions. Their immaturity prompts them to pout or shout or defend so strongly that it illustrates how sorely lacking they are in the finely tuned skills necessary for healthy relationships. Yet, let's not be too negative in assessing children.

We can say yes to a child's personal management skills because children *can* learn appropriateness in their expressions and attitudes once they receive consistent encouragement to understand right from wrong. Children begin life with unsophisticated habits, yet there is always the capacity to refine those habits upward.

What do you believe in this respect? What evidence have you seen that validates the notion that children can in fact be taught emotionally healthy skills? (For instance, "I have seen times when my son has calmed down and changed his angry expressions to cooperation.")

_____

_____

_____

Children can be taught emotional competence. It takes time and persistence, but it is certainly a reasonable goal to maintain for a child. They are not forever doomed to a life of immature emotional expressions.

Now look back upon your own childhood. How much encouragement did you receive during your developmental years to sift out the meaning and direction of your emotions? Your communicational goals? Your attitudes in relationships? It is at this juncture that most depressed people admit a very minimal training. We often hear such statements as "We rarely took the necessary time to explore feelings in our home," or "I was told what to do, but I wasn't really encouraged to draw my own conclusions about deeply personal matters."

Most depressed people did not learn in their childhood years the intricacies involved in emotional management. Just as they needed someone to teach them to read or to ride a bicycle, they needed someone to patiently guide them through the complications of emotional experiences. Consider for a moment some examples of the many issues children need to be trained to manage:

- how to respond confidently to another person's statements of rejection

- when to be forgiving of another person's insensitivities

- how to express their frustrations clearly while also being respectful of others' feelings

INADEQUACY FEELINGS SETTLE IN

- how to accept personal failures without unnecessary guilt

- how to establish boundaries without also seeming rejecting or rigid

- how to establish a responsible, loving rapport with an individual of the opposite gender

- how to let qualities like contentment and peacefulness be a natural part of their personalities

- how to avoid the pitfalls of pride

- how to find a balance between the desire to have peer approval and the need to be independently secure

- how to manage the feelings of insecurity that are a natural part of being a kid

The list could be much longer, but you get the point. Many elements necessary for successful relating need to be introduced to a person in the first eighteen years of life. A task for the parents is to consistently guide the growing child through these issues, encouraging introspection, helping the child to develop a strong discerning mind.

As you reflect back on your early years, how were personal matters explored in your family? (For instance, "My mother was willing to talk about my emotions, though sometimes I think she didn't know exactly what to say," or "In our home, we just did what we were told with very little discussion.")

_____

_____

_____

How about in your adult years? What encouragement have you had (or not had) to sift through the meaning of your emotions? (For instance, "My spouse doesn't like to get into anything that requires deep thought.")

_____

_____

_____

In both childhood and adulthood, most depressed people can recall a familiar trend of being discouraged from developing a lasting feeling of adequacy. When an emotion is expressed or if there is a personal problem to be resolved, they are told what to do. They are offered advice, often from well-intentioned persons, but they are not allowed to struggle with their own opinions. They are not encouraged to look inwardly for strength and direction.

In times, then, when that inner strength needs to be utilized the most, there is little "know-how" regarding the intricacies of emotional management. The result is a sense of emotional incompetence that sets the stage for depression.

For instance, as Suzette and Dr. Minirth continued their consultations, she confessed, "As a girl I didn't have it so bad. Daddy wasn't really a nurturing person, but I know he loved me. He was uncomfortable with exploring personal problems, so I just learned to steer clear of him whenever I needed advice. Now Mother, she was a different story. I could talk with her about almost anything and she always had advice to give. She wasn't bashful in that category at all."

"She gave you advice, but did she stimulate you to claim ownership of your own ideas and philosophies?" asked Dr. Minirth. "By that I mean did she know when to stay out of the advising capacity in order to give you the room to decide for yourself what you believed?"

"I guess I haven't thought about it quite like that, but now that you mention it, I don't think she ever really asked for my input. Our discussions were more of her telling and me listening."

Can you relate? What experiences have you had in which you were told what to do without necessarily finding your own solution? (For instance, "My husband is too impatient to listen to my emotions. He has very cut-and-dried advice on how I should respond to people.")

1. _____

_____

2. _____

_____

Can you see how the lack of emotional competence can result in feelings of inadequacy and depression? When you are not allowed to explore deeply your own ideas or philosophies, you can eventually conclude that the solutions to your problems are out of reach. You can even feel paralyzed in your responses to unwanted experiences. When the number or intensity of those experiences is at an overload you can collapse in depression.

But let's hold on to hope. You can break the cycle of emotional incompetence by developing *contemplative thinking*. You can learn that your feelings of inadequacy do not have to be permanently entrenched. You can commit to figuring out your problems one by one until you forge a direction in life choices that generally leads you toward healthy emotional and relational responses.

Take Suzette's circumstances. She originally sought counseling because of major burnout stemming from the emptiness caused by poor moral choices and social rejections. Because of her failures, she had concluded that she had nothing good to offer anyone new in her life. But through Dr. Minirth's encouragement not to be so black-and-white in her thinking, she admitted she did indeed possess some pleasant social skills. She was encouraged to continue seeking dates and friendships that would keep her from becoming too isolated.

Knowing she had been prone to sexual promiscuity and also to temper outbursts in her past, Suzette used several counseling sessions to explore why she had the inclinations she did. Through new insights, she learned to monitor carefully her vulnerabilities regarding male affirmation and conflict resolution, and as she mastered new patterns of relating she began realizing she *could* choose successful responses to people.

For instance, she learned to recognize the signs when a man was becoming too suggestive sexually, and she rehearsed how she would say no, even to the point of ending the relationship if necessary. Likewise, she admitted her tendency to hold in frustrated feelings with friends and coworkers. Knowing how her stored-up emotions created depression, she resolved to be more immediate in expressing needs with key people. Her initiative in these matters helped her feel less inadequate, proving that she did not have to get swept away by unwanted circumstances.

Her counseling sessions taught Suzette one major fact: Her problem was one not of incompetence but of lack of insight, awareness, and application. She began reorienting her thoughts about herself by acknowledging that she had always had the capacity for decent living, but she needed the inner initiative to know how to integrate that capacity into daily choices. Her ability to change, then, was directly proportional to her willingness to see herself as a competent person who could successfully address her needs.

As you survey the areas in your life unnecessarily burdened by feelings of inadequacy, what are five or six key adjustments you can make in your responses to your life's demands? (For instance, "I need to hold more firmly to my moral principles rather than letting others determine for me what I believe.")

1. _____

2. _____

3. _____

4. _____

5. _____

6. _____

As you begin to act upon your sense of competence, you will adjust in another major area: your tendency toward dependencies.

Breaking Dependency's Hold

When you consider the word *dependency*, what comes to mind? Often this trait carries a stereotyped image of a weak, wishy-washy person who waits for others' handouts just to survive. To be sure, that is dependency, but by no means is this trait so one-dimensional. For the purpose of understanding your emotions, we can describe dependency as the tendency to allow your inner stability to be determined by external circumstances.

Perhaps you can recall a recent occasion when you said: "It's hard to have a good outlook on life when people are treating me so badly," or "I was having a perfectly good day until . . ." If so, you have been caught in the web of dependency. You have assumed you can feel content or pleasant or secure only after circumstances give you what you want.

Before we proceed further, let's underscore that dependency is not always abnormal, nor is it necessarily wrong. Each personality is wired to respond positively to affirming input or negatively to rejecting input. Human nature is such that individuals live most effectively when connected satisfactorily to others. So dependency per se is not a problem to be rid of. It is excessive dependency that keeps a person feeling inadequate, creating an inclination toward depression.

How closely do your feelings of depression reflect a tendency to let your mood be dictated by your circumstances? To get an idea, check the following statements that apply to you:

___ I feel acceptable only when I get large doses of affirmation from others.

___ I cringe when I sense rejection is forthcoming.

___ When I'm around confident people I repeatedly wish I could be more that way.

___ I have noticed over the past months and years that I am cynical toward people even before they give me a reason to feel that way.

___ Lately, I have been more guarded about the things I will reveal about myself.

___ Criticism from others can send me into an emotional tailspin.

___ I want more rewarding relationships, but I'm beginning to conclude they don't exist.

___ Sometimes I alter my words to suit the person I am with.

___ I become easily embarrassed or shy when my shortcomings are discovered.

___ I find myself waiting for someone to come along and rescue me from my misery.

You will notice that each of the statements implies a tendency to let your mood be determined by something outside yourself. As you sink into depression you will almost inevitably experience a rise in this tendency. If you checked five or more statements, you are probably so intent on getting your emotional stability from unpredictable outside sources that you are virtually asking to be depressed. Sad reality shows that (1) other people cannot read your mind sufficiently to know how to *make* you feel good about yourself, and (2) even if others were able to read your mind, they would not necessarily be inclined to fix your problems.

Consider the many times your mood has been excessively tied to an event or to a person's treatment of you. What are some of the most common circumstances that get you down? (For instance,

"When my spouse acts cranky it sends me into a bad mood," or "When I am unappreciated at work I become very discouraged.")

1. _____
2. _____
3. _____
4. _____

When you woke up this morning you probably did not sit on the side of your bed thinking, "I'm going to hand over my emotional stability to everyone else in my life today." In other words, dependency is not typically a conscious plan. Yet, dependency can be so habitual that it can occur without your immediate conscious awareness. This is generally the case because this trait is natural to every human from earliest life, and it tends to remain as a powerful, even destructive, force in life until you are trained to maintain it in proper perspective.

On the day you were born your dependency was displayed. As soon as you entered the world you cried to be held and affirmed. When you sensed a comforting message, you became calm. If you were ignored, you screamed, demanding nurturing attention. Your emotional stability was almost completely dictated by your surroundings. You were that dependent.

As the months and years passed, you became more sophisticated in managing your responses to your world, yet you continued in your craving for affirmation. Just as you did on that first day of life, you wanted to consistently hear "You can feel safe because I'm here to love you and protect you." As you received proper doses of personal confirmation, your emotions stabilized. But in affirmation's absence you struggled to find your inner value. Most depression sufferers look upon the past and recall that those inborn cravings for affirmation were lacking in one or more major relationships. Perhaps a parent was condescending or found it hard to express love, or perhaps you felt estranged from a spouse or a brother or a work associate. In your mind you had ongoing questions regarding your standing with others to the extent that you increasingly felt defeated and inadequate.

Suzette reflected with Dr. Minirth about her feelings of security in her early years. "Mother did what she could to provide security at home. She worked during part of my childhood, and I remember missing her some during those stretches of time but not excessively so. It was my relationship with my father, though, that kept me feeling most insecure."

"Was he openly hostile toward you?"

"I wouldn't put it that way, although he *could* crush me with just a look. Most of the time, I just wished I could have some involvement with him. He was strict in some ways, and I always knew I'd better toe the line to keep away from his anger. But for the most part, he was very detached. I wondered frequently if I really mattered to him."

She continued her explanation by saying that she had been on a hunt most of her life for male affection. When she had a boyfriend in her teens or twenties she tended toward clingy, possessive behavior. After her divorce she had such a yearning to know that she was lovable that she frequently disregarded her traditional values and let herself be used sexually by men, all in the hope that she would receive the affirmation that had never been fully hers.

What incidences from your past have a direct bearing today on your feelings of inadequacy? (For instance, "I rarely felt accepted by the social group," or "My father's love was tainted by the fact that he was so temperamental.")

_____

_____

_____

Part of your recovery from depression will be tied to your ability to restructure your habits regarding dependency. Know that you had a God-given worth on the day you were born, and though it would have been appropriate for your significant people to have communicated that worth to you, if they failed to do so it does not make the fact of your worth any less true. Your adequacy is not given to you by fallible humans, though you may wish they could somehow magically bestow it upon you. Adequacy comes from God Himself. He gave you reasoning, free will, competence. It is your privilege to use it as you choose, and it does not have to hinge on others' recognition of it.

Hold on to the fact that others are not responsible for making you feel secure. Yes, it is pleasing and helpful when others choose to affirm you, but don't ascribe to others a godlike power to dictate whether you can be emotionally stable or mentally optimistic today. Notice how this works in the following scenarios:

- Your mother never could understand why you handle decisions as you do. But instead of pleading your case or defending your position, decide to let her have her opinions even as you continue steadfastly in your own mannerisms.

- Your spouse has no desire to hear about (much less understand) your emotions. You don't want to get caught in a pleading battle, so you can declare how you feel while refraining from salesmanship.

- Your children have a habit of talking back when you give instructions, but instead of joining in the griping, you can calmly state the consequences to potential disobedience, then let the children decide what move is next.

- Your coworker is critical about people (including you) behind their backs. Rather than adjusting to avoid those criticisms, you can choose to live in your own appropriate preferences and let her think whatever she wants.

As you consider areas in your life in which your mood could be more independently directed, what scenarios come to mind? (For instance, "I can determine to be less phony with some of my social acquaintances.")

1. _____

2. _____

3. _____

What positive traits will be more prominent as you disconnect from others' moods? (For instance, "I'd worry much less about what I should say in the presence of my friends.")

1. _____

2. _____

3. _____

Let's be as realistic as possible in describing your goals to be more emotionally independent. First, to be your own person you will need to put lots of thought into your beliefs about the healthy life. What traits do you want to lead the way in your personality? What good qualities are you committed to, even in the midst of others' displays of undesirable traits? What seems to be a reasonable response when others are rejecting or angry or aloof?

As Suzette discussed with Dr. Minirth how she would break depression's hold, she admitted, "I've always been able to say what I *don't* want in my life. . . . I don't want rejection or disillusionment or temper outbursts. But I can't say that I've really thought hard enough about what I *do* want."

"When you're stuck in depression and its accompanying feelings of inadequacy," explained Dr. Minirth, "you can easily find yourself hoping that others will pull you out of your hole. But based on our discussions I think we could conclude that is not a very secure way to live. You can't just assume someone will step forward as your rescuer. But you need not collapse in despair. *You* have a good mind that can discern healthy traits, and you also have the skills to put those traits into play—even if others choose not to go along."

A smile broke out on Suzette's face. "It's so refreshing to hear you say those things. I've wanted to believe that I was adequate to make good choices, but I've never been that sure of myself."

"It's my job to work myself out of a job." Dr. Minirth smiled. "What I'm saying about your inner strength I really believe. My hope for you is that you will build a base of successes so you can experience joy in your life, making me less necessary." He then asked Suzette to enumerate some of the qualities she would like to see more frequently in her personality.

How about you? What character goals could you aim toward that are reasonably within reach? (For instance, "I'd like to be more confident and less apologetic about my needs," or "I want to be less critical and more uplifting.")

1. _____
2. _____
3. _____
4. _____

In what circumstance will you most commonly need to focus your growth efforts? (For instance, "I need patience most when I'm with my kids," or "I need to be less defensive around my gossipy neighbor.")

1. _____
2. _____
3. _____

Who in your life will be uncooperative or nonunderstanding as you independently choose to put your positive traits into action? (For instance, "My spouse thinks it's weak that I read self-help books, but I'll just let him think that even as I press on in my growth efforts.")

1. _____
2. _____
3. _____

Depressed people are forever waiting for others to set the pace for emotional stability, when it really is not necessary that they do so. Set your own pace! Be an initiator, not a reactor. And don't make it your job to force others to understand why you do what you do.

This idea led to significant insights for Suzette. "When I've been with peers, I've had a habit of becoming frustrated, waiting for others to show interest in me. Of course, when I just lay back and acted timid I virtually asked for the very rejection I didn't want. My goal at this point is to be more direct in sharing myself with others. I'll let folks know there is something desirable in my personality by acting like I like myself."

Small but significant changes occurred. For instance, a coworker had a habit of lobbing sarcastic remarks Suzette's way. So instead of quietly fuming, she chose to talk to her about maintaining a more respectful atmosphere at work. In addition, rather than waiting for others to befriend her, she took the initiative to invite potential friends to join her for lunch.

"I'm *very* encouraged for you," Dr. Minirth said, smiling. "Let's assume in advance that you'll not achieve perfection in your efforts to connect with others; no one ever becomes perfect. But let's also assume that as you choose to act more independently, your life will have more successes than it did when you just waited for someone else to make you feel good."

At this point, let's be very pragmatic. You know that you will probably set yourself up for disappointment if you declare today: "From now on I'm going to be less dependent and more decisive in all my interactions." Such a statement is too broad. Pare it down into a more reasonable goal. Think in terms of brief increments of time. Be very specific regarding the independent goals you can put into practice. For instance:

- When I'm socializing with my friends this evening from 7:00 to 9:00, I'm going to choose not to worry about saying the "correct" thing. I'm going to let me be me, even if I don't fit their mold.

- Sunday afternoon when I am visiting my sister-in-law, I am going to choose kindness even when she speaks irritably like she often does. My mood will not be determined by her erratic emotions.

- For the first hour this evening when my spouse and I come together after work, I am going to commit to pleasantness regardless of my spouse's mood. This will not be a phony act; it will genuinely be the way I want to be.

- I know I'm going to be talking with my teenage daughter this afternoon about a discipline matter she won't like. I'll choose to stand my ground calmly without coercion and maintain my composure even if she goes into a rage.

Do you get the idea? Your feelings of inadequacy are usually caused when you fail to take the reins for your own actions, letting your mood be determined by others. That does not have to be. By developing an awareness of your unique vulnerable moments, and by determining who you can be in response to those circumstances, you can set into motion some realistic goals for coping. It may not be easy or natural, but then what major adjustment is? Search yourself to determine what you believe is a reasonable way to respond to unreasonableness. Be realistic enough to know that you will encounter many undesirable situations every week; then be wise enough to consider often your mature responses to those situations.

What are some of your recurring circumstances that tend to create troubled emotions for you? (For instance, "My spouse quickly invalidates me when I have a point to make.") Make a list of the most common:

1. _____
2. _____
3. _____
4. _____
5. _____

Now go back through each of the circumstances you just cited and determine a reasonable healthy response to each of those circumstances. (For instance, "When my spouse interrupts me, I'll not get sidetracked by his/her argumentativeness, but I will noncoercively stick to my beliefs.")

1. _____
2. _____
3. _____
4. _____
5. _____

What effect will this decisiveness have on your feelings of inadequacy and depression? (For instance, "I'll be less worried about others' judgment before I initiate my plans," or "I'll be acting upon a real belief in myself.")

1. _____
2. _____
3. _____

Depression is fed by a sit-and-wait approach to life. Wait for others to tell you you're okay. Wait for others to give you permission to be decisive. Wait for others to be respectful before you can tame your frustrations. But as you break from your depressive tendencies, you will make decisions and build behavioral habits around your growing belief that you have adequacy to meet the challenges of trying circumstances. You no longer have to feel like a yo-yo on the end of someone else's string, but you can stake out your own beliefs and determine how you will translate those beliefs into change one circumstance at a time.

5

Coming to Terms with Abuse

Step 5. Refuse to be a perpetual victim of past or present abuse.

Imagine that you are lined up as a participant in a 100-meter race. Competitors are all your age and weight, so there are no particular physical disadvantages to burden you. One element distinguishes you from the group though. Locked around your ankle is a fifty-pound ball and chain, so you have no choice but to run with it. On your mark, get set, go! How are you going to do? Not only are you going to finish last but running the race will be strenuous and painful.

If you have ever contended with depression you will readily relate to the ball and chain analogy. From all outward appearances you may seem to be on a level ground with your peers, yet you have a cumbersome emotional load holding you back, keeping you from progressing with the pack. In a very high percentage of depression cases, that ball and chain is a history of abuse. Whether you suffered abuse years ago as a child or fairly recently as an adult, you can feel loaded down with tension because of an abuser's insensitivity.

If you have experienced abuse, in whatever form, it is not a matter to be considered lightly. It cannot be shrugged off, nor can it be resolved by just talking about it a time or two. Abusive circumstances must be openly acknowledged with the understanding that these circumstances have created behavioral and emotional tendencies that will require major examination and restructuring. Left unresolved, depression, anger, and anxiety are virtual certainties. But when the abuse is successfully explored, you can expect to be freed to a normal, emotionally healthy life.

Melissa had originally sought counseling with Dr. Carter because of an eating disorder. Since her last child was born more than three years earlier she had put on fifty pounds more than she had previously carried. She was diagnosed with depression, and, after several sessions, Melissa learned that her overeating was secondary to the mishandling of her emotions. She and Dr. Carter determined that they would set aside the focus on her weight problem until they had more fully explored why she felt depressed.

About the sixth time she met with him, Melissa said, "I haven't said anything to you about this because I've never been comfortable talking about it, but I was sexually abused by my older brother when I was a girl."

Encouraged that she had mustered the boldness to reveal this fact about herself, Dr. Carter spoke calmly, "It's not surprising that you would want to keep such a problem a secret. I can think of few things that are more humiliating than to have experienced sexual abuse." Both paused quietly for a moment, then he continued, "If you are willing, I'd like to hear some of the circumstances surrounding your experiences."

Feeling relieved that the ice had been broken, Melissa explained, "I was about nine or ten years old the first time Rob approached me. It was in our basement where we often played in the summer when it was too hot to go outside. He was three years older than me, and I always thought he was some sort of bully. He started by making sexually suggestive statements that I didn't understand, then he exposed himself. This happened several times, and then at night he'd come into my bedroom and molest me. I was way too young to know what to do. I wanted to tell my mother, but I was too embarrassed, so I just kept it to myself and tried not to be alone with Rob."

"How long did this continue?" asked Dr. Carter.

"At least two years. It didn't happen every day or even every week, but it was often enough that it kept me on pins and needles wondering when it might happen again. I really learned to hate my brother and to this day we don't get along. But I also felt guilty because I thought I should be able to stop it and I knew I shouldn't hate."

"Let's establish right now that you were too confused and naive to have known how to handle this problem. A nine- or ten-year-old girl normally has her mind on much simpler and more innocent matters. What Rob did put you on overload. You don't need to hold to any guilt over this."

"In my mind I know that, but my emotions tell me otherwise," she explained.

"Where were your parents when all this was going on?"

"Well, Mother was the one to put a stop to it when she found him spying on me one night when I was in bed. He didn't confess to anything and I didn't tell her the full story, but she knew he was always rough toward me and she kept a lot closer eye on him. I used that incident to tell him that if he ever touched me in an uncomfortable way again I'd tell everything. No more sexual abuse happened but he still put terror in me just through sheer meanness. The happiest day of my childhood was the day he left for college."

Terror. That's a good word to use to describe the feeling that can come upon an abused person. If you have ever been abused you know how your emotions can run the course through hate, fear, confusion, guilt, panic. Often abuse victims become so emotionally overwhelmed that they eventually learn temporarily to disassociate during the abusive experience. They feel so helpless that their immediate defense is to zone out.

But that disassociation cannot last forever. At some point, the emotions that have been buried begin to wear the person down, often in the form of depression. The shame, insecurity, anger, and bitterness cannot be permanently contained no matter how hard the victim tries to keep up the appearance of normalcy. To overcome the aftereffects of abuse, the victim will have to assess honestly what has been done.

As you consider the factors involved in your depression, you may need to become very honest with yourself about your feelings associated with past mistreatments. First, let's ask: What is abuse? Abuse goes beyond the actual act of sexual manipulation or extreme physical mistreatment. Abuse can be defined as harshly insensitive treatment that inflicts long-standing emotional pain continuing well beyond the actual event. All families can experience conflict that creates a temporary experience of strong emotion. But in abusive relationships the discomfort is so penetrating that it significantly inhibits that person's ability to respond to otherwise normal friction or challenges.

Have you suffered abuse? Do not be afraid to admit it openly. If you did, you did not plan for it to happen or participate in its initiation. You did not know what to do, feeling emotionally paralyzed and perplexed.

Look over the following list of abuse indicators and check the ones that apply to you:

___ I have received very insulting treatment and then been told that I'd better not let anyone else know it.

___ Someone else has engaged me in sexual misconduct before I knew how I was supposed to respond, or even what was really happening.

___ Because of mistreatment, I have harbored a bitter feeling inside for quite some time.

___ Others have been so accusing toward me that I have a pattern of accepting blame for problems I didn't create.

___ Through earlier conflicts, I learned that it is easier just to hold my painful feelings inside.

___ I seem to be far too defensive now when someone confronts me or tries to talk about my deficiencies.

___ I have learned that a good way to avoid pain is to avoid people.

___ Others have been manipulative toward me, leaving me bewildered about the best way to respond.

___ Sometimes I feel very confused about what normal relating really is.

___ There have been times when I have responded to harsh treatment with out-of-bounds behavior (substance abuse, promiscuity, eating disorder, temper outbursts, etc.).

___ There are memories of past mistreatment that are so embarrassing that I try to create a false favorable impression rather than reveal the truth.

___ Trusting others is very difficult or unnatural for me.

Checking even one of the above statements could indicate that you have received mistreatment that would be considered abusive. The more you checked the more likely it is that you have been emotionally scarred.

What inner conflicts stand out for you most that could indicate a history of abuse? (For instance, "I am easily angered even when reasons for it don't exist," or "I am very guilt driven.")

_____

_____

_____

As Melissa described her symptoms of depression to Dr. Carter she revealed many of the signs most common to this problem—withdrawal, repressed emotions, and poor boundaries being most prominent. So he asked, "When is the earliest time you remember holding back your emotions and needs?"

"My mother tells me that I was a real free-spirited kid, particularly prior to school. I can remember how I took school very seriously, so I suppose I lost some of my carefree nature around age six or seven. But I very distinctly remember when Rob began abusing me that I felt such a sense of shame I just shut down. I may have still appeared outwardly friendly or cooperative, but inside I was becoming a very different, less secure person."

This account by Melissa had a very familiar ring to Dr. Carter because he had heard numerous similar descriptions from abused persons. "When were you first aware of feeling depressed?" he asked.

"You might think it was while the abuse was happening," she replied, "but it's only been in the last couple of years that I've really felt so down that I couldn't get back up. Early in my marriage I didn't have much trouble being intimate with my husband, both physically and emotionally, but now I'd prefer he just stay away." She hesitated, then added, "But I don't *really* want him to stay away because I still love him." She appeared flustered as tears began forming in her eyes.

As she and the doctor continued their discussions she disclosed that she had been feeling increasingly different from women friends.

"They all seem to have it more together than I do. I just feel like someone's old dirty laundry."

Often the effects of abuse take years to play out in your personality. At the time the abuse occurs the victim can at least cling to the hope that one day it will end. The victim often thinks: "I'm not sure how to get out of my troubles but I just know I'll be free from this some day." Often it is that hope for release that keeps the person sane. But then when the abuse is past, new awarenesses can surface. Emotions or reactions that had been suppressed begin to resurface, and at that time the tendency toward depression or anxiety can increase. The abused person often experiences depression while in the midst of the circumstances, but the depression does not go away when the abuse ceases. Time alone does not heal all wounds.

That is what had happened to Melissa. She told Dr. Carter, "I felt very dirty as a girl because I was so confused, not just because of the sexual abuse but also because of the hate inside me. I found after getting married that I was very touchy when conflicts arose. My husband tells me I give him a dollar's worth of anger when he does something wrong when a nickel's worth would do."

"You're experiencing what is called displacement. At the time you experienced abuse you wanted to unlock all your emotion, but much remained bottled inside. Now your emotions related to the past are being played out on a new stage with different players. You'll experience less current distress when you make sense of your feelings regarding your abuse."

You *can* get beyond the grip of abusive memories, but to do so you really have to want to be different and commit to a new way of thinking. That is what Melissa chose to do, with Dr. Carter's help. The depression you feel makes sense, given the fact that you have endured what you should never have had to experience. But don't assume you are stuck with those depressed feelings forever. Now is the time for you to commit to a new approach to yourself and your life. Several factors can help you accomplish lasting change.

Refuse to Be Secretive About Your Abuse

Receiving abuse is painful enough. But to add insult to injury, abused persons are usually caught in the trap of having to keep quiet about the problem. Held down by tremendous embarrassment and confusion, many victims can go years without revealing to anyone the extent of their experiences. During that time the suppressed feelings become so powerful that they can take over the personality. Bitterness builds. Insecurity grows, along with doubt. Self-directed shame becomes the norm. Because they do not expose their difficulties, they lack the benefit of objective analysis, leaving emotions to run rampant with little forward direction.

To break the emotional hold (and its resulting depression) associated with abuse, you will need to disclose your feelings to someone who can support and help you. For instance, if you are in an abusive marriage you are doing yourself and your spouse no favors by telling no one. Bring a responsible person into the loop, whether it be a counselor, a close friend, a minister, or a family member. You need help and so does the abuser. Ask for it.

Your supportive relationship can serve the function of encouraging you and bringing reason to a very unreasonable set of circumstances. Let others be an uplifting presence, just as you would be if the role were reversed. (It is often easier to be an encouragement giver than an encouragement receiver, but put down your pride and let someone in, regardless of the short-term awkwardness you may feel.)

Some people are sheepish about exposing their problems. What about you? What feeling does talking about your problems create in you? (For instance, "I'd feel dirty telling someone else about my abuse," or "I'm normally in control; revealing my problems would cause me to feel out of control.")

_____

_____

_____

_____

Consider the alternative of ongoing suppression regarding your abuse. What will *that* do to you? (For instance, "It will keep me imprisoned by my sense of loneliness.")

_____

_____

_____

_____

There are numerous excuses you could fall back on to keep you from being open:

• What's done is done. I can't change the past.

• It happened so long ago that it's no longer relevant.

• I doubt that anyone would really understand my problems.

• No one wants to hear my complaints. It would just be a bother.

• I'm not sure I could face people again after telling them about my problems. I'd be too embarrassed.

• Talking about it still can't change the pain I feel.

Which excuses are you most likely to use?

1. _____

2. _____

3. _____

The ongoing nature of your depression, though, indicates that you cannot afford to hide behind those excuses. The longer you keep your problems to yourself, the deeper the emotional scars.

Now, let's assume you determine to talk. You declare to a confidant the nature of your problems. A very natural question is likely to arise: Should I also openly confront my abuser? In most cases the answer is yes. You need to declare to the abuser that you have been hurt by the inappropriate actions and you would like to see some repentance and accountability. It is *not* your responsibility to force any changes in that person's life, but at least you will need to register your thoughts for the sake of eliminating the secrecy.

As Dr. Carter and Melissa talked about her past abuse, Melissa confessed that it would be hard to talk with Rob about the mistreatment she had received from him, yet she knew it had to be done. "In a strange way I feel like I have to protect Rob, and the longer I stay in that mind-set the stronger I feel about my past." Then pausing she added, "It's not my place to protect him. I don't want to harm him, but I don't feel like he deserves favored treatment either." Dr. Carter nodded in agreement.

Before meeting with Rob, Melissa had a long talk with her mother. (Her dad had since died.) Both cried as Melissa talked about what had happened between her and her brother years ago. "I knew that you never got along with each other," her mother cried, "but I just wished I had known the full details sooner than I did. I would have handled things very differently if I had known."

"Mother, right now I just need to hear that you understand my feelings and that you love and support me. I know you have no blame in this, but I need you to realize why I've struggled with depression for as long as I have. It's miserable keeping the memories inside like I have."

The two shared feelings of strong support and encouragement for each other, and this lifted Melissa's spirits significantly. "It's like a load of bricks was lifted off my back when I discussed it with my mother," she explained to Dr. Carter.

Confronting her brother proved to be a less than satisfying experience though. "I went to his house for the first time in several years. He was obviously expecting something uncomfortable because we just don't have casual visits."

"How did you broach the subject?"

"Well, first I told him that I had determined my life could no longer be chained to painful feelings from the past. I explained that I had lots of hang-ups and insecurities as a girl, and that much of it began when he molested me. I told him I had patterns of confusion in my life because I was never really sure if I was okay or if my feelings were legit. I talked for several minutes, and I'm afraid I may have rambled some of the time, but basically I told him that his actions had hurt me and I hoped he would get some help so he could discover how to have a more responsible life."

"Did he receive your words well?"

"Not really. He didn't deny any wrongdoing, but he didn't apologize or ask for forgiveness. My guess is that he'll go on just being Rob. But at least he and I will have an understanding that *I'm* not going to go on being the same timid little sister. I think he saw a new strength in me, and that's worth something."

The goal of open expression is not to harm but to heal. Melissa had handled her reactions well. She had discussed her past with her mother without trying to defame her brother, yet she no longer felt the need to coddle his reputation. She needed her mother's support, and though it was years later than it could have been, she received it. Melissa wisely chose not to speak maliciously to Rob. She was firm in what she had to say, yet she realized if she had become caustic she would have lowered herself to his former level, which would have been dissatisfactory.

Who do you need to talk with regarding past abuses?

_____

_____

_____

What would be the general message you would like to convey? (For instance, "I now see myself as a valuable person whose personal needs should be more clearly respected.")

_____

_____

_____

Though you cannot anticipate other people's reactions, perhaps you can anticipate how you might feel upon sharing your experiences. What benefit might there be for you? (For instance, "I'd see myself as someone who could stand equal-to-equal with others.")

_____

_____

_____

Two more thoughts:

1. You may find it very helpful before disclosing your experiences to write your thoughts in letter form. This would give you the chance to reflect carefully on the key messages you would like to convey.
2. Do not be surprised if some persons do not know how to receive your disclosures. They may doubt you or downplay your emotions' significance. Keep in mind that your goal is not to change others but to become honest and authentic.

Refuse to Cling to the Victim's Label

In the past several years, a very refreshing trend has emerged in our culture, that of being more open about formerly hidden pains. No one benefits by keeping abusive experiences secretive. Remember, when you reveal your abuse to a trusted friend you are not exposing your own inappropriateness. You are exposing your humanness and your heroic desire to be normal and healthy, and you are also demonstrating a commitment to authenticity.

But as is so often the case, when good trends emerge they can be accompanied by a downside. In the trend of openly disclosing abusive experiences, some people have strongly encouraged abused persons to cling so tightly to their victimization that it becomes the defining element in their characters. Abused persons can overlearn to interpret the world through the eyes of their abuse. For instance, if a woman is shy, she could say, "It's because my father was so harsh in his discipline." Perhaps her experiences of abuse did contribute greatly to her shyness, but is that the only reason she has this struggle?

By holding too strongly to your victimization, you can ascribe so much power to the one who has wronged you that you lose sight of your own ability to choose for yourself. You allow the abuser continually to play a role in your life even after he or she is no longer a major immediate player.

Examples of this tendency are plentiful:

- A wife whose former husband constantly berated and insulted her could say: "Because my husband was so mean-spirited, I'll never be fit for a trusting relationship again."

- A man who was treated severely as a boy by his father could say: "It's impossible for me to feel confident around authority figures. How can I be strong after the way my dad treated me?"

89

• A woman who had been sexually abused as a girl could assume: "I'll never be able to experience a normal relationship with another man."

• A person who has been severely judged and then rejected by an important peer group could think: "I'm damaged goods, and no one will ever want me as a friend again."

In each of these illustrations a very real hurt was experienced, resulting in a legitimate low feeling. But can you see the exaggeration? This is all-or-nothing thinking. There is little allowance for anything between the extremes.

Have you ever used all-or-nothing thinking in reaction to abuse? What are some examples? (For instance, "I cannot tolerate overbearing people because my father was so much that way.")

1. _____

_____

2. _____

_____

Moderate that style of thinking. What would be a less black-and-white approach in the examples you just gave? (For instance, "Though my father was very overbearing, I am no longer required to cower in the presence of such people.")

1. _____

_____

2. _____

_____

Were you a victim? Yes, abusive people seek out those they think are less powerful, and they play out their anger and insecurity upon that weaker person. It is an extreme act of indignity that you did not ask for or deserve. Are you required to wear your victim's status like a badge of distinction? No. There are many other aspects of your personality that deserve greater attention. For instance, you may be gifted with children. Perhaps you have a fun-loving side that puts people at ease. You may be a very logical, reasonable person whose value to a group is immeasurable. Make certain you are not so intent on examining your problems that you lose sight of what is right about you. Do not let someone else's impropriety define who you are. Strike a balance between confronting your pain and building on your uniqueness.

You were a victim, yes. But what positives are in your personality that should not be overlooked simply because of your abuse? (For instance, "My sense of humor keeps the family from being too negative," or "I am very supportive when someone is feeling confused.")

_____

_____

_____

During the time you received abuse, you were so concerned with mere survival and keeping your sanity that your emotional energy was spent. A habit was established that kept you thinking about your pain, your shame, your desire to be free. Once you are removed from the victimization, it is easy to remain in that same habit. Allow yourself to break from its grip. Know that you are beyond the victimizing events. Permit yourself to focus on what is good and right and responsible in your personality. See yourself as someone with something to offer.

This concept was both refreshing and difficult for Melissa. She explained, "When I meet people I have this quiet sensation that there is something very wrong with me that I can't let others know. I feel defeated and inferior even before I get very far in my relationships. I know that's behind some of my self-destructing behavior."

"So you just give in to your pain and invite trouble?" Dr. Carter asked. Melissa nodded. Speaking with conviction and encouragement in his voice, Dr. Carter said, "Melissa, I wonder what would be different if you let go of your victim's identity long enough to allow your more positive traits to become prominent?"

A look came over her face that seemed to say, "You mean I can do that?" She smiled and said, "I've always felt that I could be a very good friend. I'm very loyal, and I'll take whatever time is needed to help a friend through the day's tensions. Are you suggesting that I should see myself more in that light?"

"Of course! It is *you*, isn't it? Yes, you have pain and insecurity associated with your brother's abuse, but there is so much about you that is healthy that I'd hate to see it ignored."

Depressed persons learn that they can climb out of their emotional holes when they permit themselves to disconnect from others' unhealthiness. This disconnection is accomplished not with denial but with self-affirmation. Allow the other aspects of your personality to have preeminence rather than just caving in to the traits that have been negatively impacted by others. This leads directly to the next point.

Stand for What Is Right

In the aftermath of abuse, people can lose their spunk. Abuse has a way of draining the emotional energy from individuals, which is why abused people so easily become depressed. The result can be that these persons act less confidently on their own initiatives, they doubt themselves, they take a wait-and-see approach to life. Their sense of resolve, therefore, may be weak as they are reduced to the roles of reactors.

Have you ever noticed this tendency in yourself? Notice some common examples:

- A friend tends to be very critical, yet you tell yourself: "I've had so much stress related to critical people, I'm just going to live with it."

- Your spouse is acting moody, but you think: "At least this mood is not as bad as the uproars we are capable of." So you keep quiet.

- A person at your place of work makes sexually suggestive remarks, but, being confused about how to address the problem, you leave it alone.

- Your children are too irritable and demanding, but you don't want to make matters worse by applying boundaries, so you wearily let them wear you down.

In these scenarios, a distinct lack of resolve is shown. Such lack of resolve is often the result of abuse-related patterns of holding needs inside for fear of reprisals that might come if one is too open.

What are some common circumstances in which you tend to lack resolve? (For instance, "I've given up on telling my family my needs, so I avoid them as much as I can.")

1. _____

2. _____

3. _____

Sometimes you can develop cynical or bitter reactions to people as you grow increasingly impatient with others' insensitivity.

How might this show itself? (For instance, "Lately, I've been very free with complaining statements.")

_____

_____

_____

In the experience of abuse, the abuser sends the message: "Your needs or feelings are unimportant. *You* are unimportant." And even though the abused may balk at such wrong sentiment, when the message is communicated often enough, it penetrates the mind with the result being demotivation.

This problem was addressed by Melissa and Dr. Carter, and it proved to be a turning point in her treatment. "I've always felt I had good ideas and down-to-earth common sense," she explained, "but I've had a tendency to keep my thoughts to myself because I never felt anyone else would take me very seriously."

"We can assume that your history of feeling overwhelmed at home has a lot to do with this tendency," said Dr. Carter. "Would you agree?"

"Yes," she said. "I distinctly remember thinking that I had less of a right to speak my mind because I had this secret problem that set me apart. So I decided it would be my lot in life to be a go-with-the-flow person. But I'm not willing at this point in my life to continue in that vein."

"I like the sound of certainty in your voice. Where are you planning on making the adjustment?"

"For starters, at home," she replied. "My husband can sometimes make schedule decisions with virtually no comprehension of how it affects me. So I've got to educate him better about my needs and point him toward more acceptable alternatives."

What about you? Perhaps you were a victim of abuse in your past, but that does not require you to go along with undesirable circumstances in the present and future. Consider how you can get away from your old inhibitions and be more open about the real you. For instance, suppose you listen to people tell jokes or stories that are personally offensive and you just quietly smile and chuckle along with the group. Can you resolve to declare openly your distaste for such matters?

List several situations like this in which you could be more open about your needs:

_____

_____

_____

_____

_____

As an example, Melissa had served on a service committee with a very overbearing woman. She often came home from her meetings near tears because this person would be so condescending, "but with a smile," as Melissa would say. With her husband's encouragement, Melissa called the woman and told her that if the meetings continued in the same unpleasant manner she would have to withdraw from the committee. Melissa was amazed at herself for being so honest about her feelings, but she was even more amazed that the next several meetings had a decidedly more pleasant tone.

Though your abuse may have caused you to assume an underling's approach toward conflict resolution, you are under no obligation to maintain the habit of letting others overwhelm you. There is no need to go to the other extreme of becoming the overbearing person. That would be responding to a wrong with a wrong. But you *can* choose to hold your ground when you sense that you are slipping into strongly negative emotions.

We are back to the concept of choice again, aren't we? What will be required for you to be more resolute as you face future distasteful circumstances? (For instance, "I will need to remind myself that the person who abused me taught me improper habits but that I am under no obligation to maintain them.")

_____

_____

_____

By standing for what is right, you are behaviorally communicating: "I now realize my abuser was erroneous in treating me poorly and I can choose to rise above the false messages that were put into my mind."

6

Grief Reactions

Step 6. Allow time for natural grief to run its course.

What pleasant things do you hope for? Most of us desire similar things: a long and satisfying life, loving family ties, financial security, success for our children, acceptance, peace of mind. Whether we are consciously aware of it or not, we each have goals such as these that set the stage for emotional composure. When these goals are reasonably within sight we can be content; when they are not, our emotions go south.

Depression commonly occurs as a grief reaction over goals that fall short of personal aspirations. Something happens (sometimes it's a single event, sometimes a series of events) that creates disappointment to such a magnitude that the despairing feelings can overwhelm you. Problems seem too big. Once-reasonable expectations fail to come true. Embarrassing failure occurs. Optimistic plans come to a screeching halt.

You can tumble into the depths of sadness as you sense the things you hoped for may never be satisfactorily achieved. For instance:

- You learn that your spouse has been unfaithful, leaving a permanent scar on your marriage.

- For reasons other than infidelity, your marriage falls apart. You become separated or divorced.

- Your marriage is intact, but it is very unrewarding as you and your mate cannot come to terms with each other.

- Your spouse dies.

- Your son or daughter dies.

- A very close friend or relative dies.

- Major hopes or plans fall through, leaving you very frustrated.

- Because of a mistake, failure, or controversy, you have been cut off from former supporters.

- A person you want to love and accept you rejects you instead.

- You have lost your job and are forced to change directions in your career.

- Your son or daughter disappoints you greatly, perhaps severing ties with the family.

• As the years have passed you conclude you are not going to be the successful person you had hoped to be in your earlier years. You struggle with a midlife crisis.

Grief can be defined as the emotion of loss, typified by feelings of anguish, sorrow, regret, and longing for something that is gone. Grief is usually accompanied by reminiscing thoughts, disillusionment, feelings of failure or incompleteness, and sometimes self-pity.

Certainly it is not wrong to feel grief, just as it is not wrong to hope for pleasant things. But grief can have a way of overstaying its welcome to the extent that it becomes lodged in the personality, at which point the person contends with powerful feelings of dejection, bitterness, and inadequacy. This is when it turns into depression.

What grief experiences have you had? What losses do you find hard to accommodate? (For instance, "My spouse died a very untimely death," or "My marriage has been disastrous," or "My career goals seem way out of reach.")

_____

_____

_____

How does your grief affect your overall lifestyle? (For instance, "I've become very withdrawn," or "My sense of morality has tumbled greatly," or "I have become very cynical.")

_____

_____

_____

Let's acknowledge that you cannot expect to have *no* emotional reaction in the wake of loss. It is normal to feel discouraged or defeated or shaken when an aspiration falls apart. It is the extreme response that needs to be tempered.

To get an idea of whether your grief might lean toward the extreme, check the following items that could apply to you:

— Several months have passed since my loss, and I still cannot shake the feeling of hopelessness.

— I tend toward one extreme or the other in communicating about my grief: I either talk too much about it or I hardly discuss it at all.

— I've become too cynical when I hear others talk about the good things in their lives.

— I'm not as outgoing or as interested in others as I used to be.

— When someone shares good news with me, I find it hard to feel really enthusiastic.

— Because of my losses I find it hard to want to go on with life.

— My mind dwells on the unfairness of my loss.

— I have felt increasingly distant from God. Once-comforting spiritual truth now seems empty.

— I feel very different in comparison to others, as if my problems have made me negatively unique.

— It seems too emotionally risky to hope that my future will bring lasting happiness.

— When friends offer words of consolation, they just don't do much to cheer me up.

The above statements illustrate how people can become so ensnared in grief that it drains them of their optimism. Their losses seem so large, so disappointing, that they lose sight of their own ability to rebound and become reestablished in rewarding pursuits. If you checked four or more of the statements, you may be susceptible to major depression. You will need to determine that your feelings of loss do not reflect excessive pessimism.

As you consider how to bring balance to your grief, what personal tendencies will you need to be cautious of? (For instance, "I feel so different from others right now that I don't let myself appreciate their expressions of concern.")

Ronald talked with Dr. Minirth about the seemingly permanent feelings of despair that had settled into his life. In his early fifties, he was a professional man who had never had a problem making ends meet. The small business he owned was currently not as successful as in the past, but he was getting by.

"Lately I've just been going through the motions," he explained. "There are many things I could do to improve my quality of life, but right now I just don't care. I do what I have to do to keep my bills paid, but I don't push myself. When I'm at home in the evenings and on the weekends, I want to be left alone as much as possible. Usually I let my answering machine screen my phone calls because I don't want to mess with people. I used to be very energetic and connected with people, but now I can't muster the desire to be around anyone."

"I doubt that this happened overnight," said Dr. Minirth. "How did you get to this point?"

"Well, the last seven or eight years have been a roller-coaster ride." He frowned as he spoke. "I had been divorced from my wife after twenty-one years of marriage, but it wasn't my choice. From Day One we had problems, but we stayed together for various reasons, mostly for our kids' sake. My wife had always been at arm's length from me, but I compensated by throwing myself into work." He continued by explaining that she too had become very career-focused and eventually developed a relationship with another man who enticed her to leave the marriage for him.

"I had mixed feelings about the divorce," he told Dr. Minirth. "On one hand there was a sense of relief because the tension at home ceased, but on the other hand I had to face full force the loss of a dream. I liked being a family man." Then a smile crossed his face as he continued. "Three years later I remarried to the most wonderful woman, Debra. She was everything I had hoped for in a wife—kind, nurturing, fun-loving. We really hit it off well. My kids felt very comfortable with her, and we had a very pleasant, stress-free life."

Noting he wore no wedding band, Dr. Minirth asked, "What became of her?"

"Not quite three years into the marriage, she was diagnosed with breast cancer. It was an awful ordeal. She endured surgery and chemo treatments, and at times we dared to feel optimistic about her chances for survival. But after ten months it was over. She died." With a look of disgust on his face, Ronald shook his head and said, "A part of me died with her. It's been a year now since Debra has been gone, and I cannot get over it. I can't sleep. I don't have much appetite. I'm afraid of getting too close to anyone again. No words of consolation make any difference to me. In fact, when people say things like 'I know how you must feel,' I just want to shout back at them 'No, you don't!' The one bright spot in my adult life was snuffed out. I can't take it anymore."

Ronald's depression is a good illustration of a grief reaction that would not go away. Was he wrong to grieve the loss of Debra? Not at all, especially given the way she had rejuvenated him in the aftermath of a very disappointing prior family life. Should he be expected to get over his loss and rejoin his world in a more productive manner? Yes. Ronald was a very reasonable, likable man who had much to offer others. Though he should never be expected to ignore his pain and go on as if his problems had not occurred, he needed to allow for the fact that he could still be a very meaningful contributor in his current family and friendship relations, and he could be a source of encouragement in the future to others who could use a companion like him.

If you get pulled into ongoing depression because of a loss, you are very likely using all-or-nothing thinking. Because life cannot give full satisfaction, the reasoning goes, there is no satisfaction to be found. The grief can cause you to be so guarded, so cautious, that you feel, like Ronald, you cannot dare hope again. Though pessimistic withdrawal is not a very attractive approach to life, it may seem easier because at least you will not hurt as badly as you might if you expectantly latch on again to a new relationship or a new venture.

Have you ever thought this way? What are some examples in your life of all-or-nothing thinking? (For instance, "My son has been such a disappointment that I can't let myself feel tenderly toward him again.")

1. _____
2. _____
3. _____

What effect does this thinking have on your emotions? (For instance, "I have been dulled to any feelings of happiness," or "I use sarcasm more frequently, particularly around upbeat people.")

_____
_____
_____

Because your loss is real, you would be abnormal if you did not acknowledge it. Recognize this though: You can choose, if you want, to let your grief so permeate your emotions that you can spend years in deep dejection, or you can determine to be increasingly sensitive to strong, supportive relationships. What will it be?

To keep your grief from creating more depression than it should, there are specific steps you can follow.

Let the Grief Run Its Course

Sometimes adverse pressure to make grief go away can turn it into overpowering depression. As a general rule, people neither like to feel dejected nor like to see someone else feel that way. When an agonizing emotion such as grief is displayed, powerful messages may come forward: "Let's get you beyond this problem so we can all go back to normal."

Do you remember as a child falling and scraping your elbow? What words did you hear as your wound was being tended to? "Don't worry; everything's going to be just fine." Not bad words for a child to hear. But can you see how many people take the same approach when the pain is more severe, more threatening?

As an example, we are familiar with a forty-year-old woman who had gone to the funeral of a two-year-old neighborhood girl who had died of a rare childhood disease. For days afterward she had cried and cried, so a friend inquired about the nature of her grief and was told: "Eighteen years ago I gave birth to a little girl who died within twenty-four hours. I was completely devastated, but my family insisted that I should be a trouper and hold my head up high. No one ever talked with me about it because I had to be strong. We didn't even give the baby a family burial." The death of the neighborhood girl brought back the memories she had been trained to block out.

Most people like life in neat packages. Sadness and despair are uncomfortable and cannot be neatly packaged. Yet, that fact does not stop many from trying to package those emotions anyway. Consider some examples:

- Right after the funeral of a loved one, you are told: "The best thing you can do is get on with your normal routine."

- When you tell a friend about a major disappointment related to your son or daughter, someone advises: "All you can do is pray about it and then not let it bother you."

- As you are bewildered in knowing what to do after losing your job, a friend says: "Think of it this way; that job you had wasn't going to get you very far anyway."

- When you take a risk and share with someone the disappointment you feel in your marriage, you hear: "I don't know how you've lived with that guy anyway. Why don't you just leave?"

Usually people are well-intentioned as they make these statements, but in their eagerness to tie down your feelings in order to move on to friendlier subjects, you can feel as if you have been stepped on in a most vulnerable place.

Has this ever happened to you? What statements have you heard (from others, from within yourself) that represent an attempt to squelch your feelings of loss? (For instance, "I've been told that the longer I sulk about my loss, the more I'm going to make everyone around me miserable.")

_____

_____

_____

When you feel pressure to hurry and get over your grief, what impact does it leave on you? (For instance, "It makes me feel all the more lonely.")

_____

_____

_____

Grief cannot be legislated. It is impossible to declare that you're going to replace it with more positive reactions. Instead, allow your grief to exist. It is normal, even necessary, to express your feelings to trusted friends. For a time you *need* to admit your bewilderment, your uncertainty, your anger. In doing so, you are avoiding the grave mistake of responding to your problems with a machinelike precision. You are showing yourself to be the full human that you are.

When you attempt to force yourself to become grief-free, you are only compounding your problems. So be real. Ask yourself: What disappointments am I having to face? Why am I angry or disillusioned? What is in my future that scares me? What insecurities now exist in me that have not been there before?

In allowing your grief to run its course, what would you have to admit about yourself that you'd really rather keep to yourself? (For instance, "I have a hard time telling people how insecure my loss has made me feel.")

_____

_____

_____

Ronald had experienced two major losses, very different from each other in some respects, but similar in the isolation they caused him to feel. In the aftermath of his divorce, he felt publicly humiliated because he knew his reputation would suffer. He had lost his dream for a successful family, and he had lost some of his stature among acquaintances. It was not his style to admit how much this hurt him, so he would cover his grief by shrugging and saying: "If people can't accept me now, it doesn't bother me; it's their loss." In portraying a false bravado, he isolated himself from others because he could not bear to show how weak he felt.

When his second wife died, he thought: "I don't want to be a nuisance to people. They've got enough problems without having to hear me whine about mine."

Dr. Minirth asked Ronald to write out his feelings in two separate letters, one to his first wife and one to his second, with the purpose of expressing to each how hurt he felt because of his separation from them. He explained, "Don't hold back what you feel. If you recall feelings of betrayal or embarrassment or love, I want you to put it all in your letters." They agreed that he would read them to the doctor on his next visit.

Three weeks passed before Ronald returned. He had canceled one appointment, and he explained to Dr. Minirth, "When I sat down at my computer to type out each letter I was unprepared for the emotion that would hit me. In both cases I expressed how badly I wanted to love and to be loved. A sense of emptiness overcame me as I realized that this feeling has been inside me since I was a boy wondering if I could ever please my parents. I've been enough of an achiever through the years to hide my hurt behind my performance successes. But I've never admitted until now how desperately I've wanted to feel special to someone and how it hurt that I couldn't have that." Right there in Dr. Minirth's office, Ronald wept like a child as he admitted that he still felt like a needy boy.

By letting your emotions be known, you can have a frame of reference for future adjustments. For instance, Ronald's depression was a direct result of unconfessed pain, but once he admitted what he needed, he could begin to make plans to build stronger, more rewarding ties to people who could know better how to love and encourage him.

If you have felt stuck in your depression, try the following:

1. Write your feelings of pain and loss in a letter form. Include in it anything that you have felt associated with your loss: your anger, your dashed dreams, your forgiveness, your loneliness. Let it all be communicated.
2. Read your letter to a trusted friend or counselor or minister. Openly claim ownership to your feelings, even if it seems out of character for you to expose your humanness this way.
3. Plan follow-up discussions with the same person. This would be for the purpose of keeping an honest update regarding the reality of your feelings.

4. Slowly begin considering how you can plan ways to become temporarily unstuck from your grief. For instance, it may involve the planning of a social outing or visiting a friend who needs your encouraging support just as you have needed the same in the past.

Which of these four steps will be the most difficult for you? (For instance, "It's hard for me to tell someone how deeply I hurt.")

_____

_____

By letting your grief run its course, how could your depression be softened? (For instance, "I'd feel less pressure to have perfect emotional composure.")

_____

_____

_____

Openness can be a good first step toward resolving the seemingly impossible task of moving forward.

Accept the Inevitability of Loss

When grief turns into major depression, it is almost universally accompanied by statements of extreme disbelief:

- "Why does something this bad have to happen to me?"

- "This is the worst possible timing for me to be dealing with such a problem."

- "I've already had enough setbacks in my life; this is more than I can handle."

- "I've tried so hard to live right. It's just not fair that life only gives me curveballs."

- "I can't imagine that anything good can come from this."

Adding strength to these statements is the fact that there is often a strong element of truth or legitimacy to them. There is no rhyme or reason regarding who suffers intensely and who does not. Sometimes individuals do not just *seem* to feel more burdened with problems as compared to others; they genuinely *are* more burdened.

How might this be the case with you? Are there genuine burdens that have caused you to suffer intensely? (For instance, "For the past several years, I've been severely strapped financially; now my latest illness has made matters much worse.")

_____

_____

_____

Whether you realize it or not, you hold in your mind ideas about normalcy and you often weigh circumstances to determine how close to the norm you are. Interestingly, the norms people hold vary greatly depending on cultural factors, socioeconomic status, family history, and educational level. For instance, an executive may grieve a job loss differently from an hourly contract worker. When your life presents circumstances out of the norm, you can inwardly protest: "Wait! Something is very foul here! Let's get things restructured so I can avoid this abnormality!" To repeat an earlier thought, it is not unhealthy to want pleasantness, yet the more you insist on it the more powerfully you can fall into depressive episodes.

Let us very delicately underscore an unpleasant fact. Loss is an unavoidable part of life. Death, rejection, illness, failure, disappointment—these things cannot be factored out of any life. You are very right to agonize over the meaning of it all or to struggle with the best ways to respond to it. But by all means, make room for it because it *will* happen.

The chief benefit for accepting the inevitability of loss is the removal of shock from your ongoing emotional response to life. Not that shock is always wrong; it usually accompanies grief reactions in the early stages. But you can exercise a denial of reality if you cling to shock to the degree that you wish to do the impossible act of rewriting events that cannot be undone.

It was perpetual shock that kept Ronald caught in his depression. Long after his divorce he would shake his head as he spoke to friends, "How could she be so rejecting toward me? Maybe I've never been the perfect family man but I'm sure not the ogre she made me out to be!" These statements were very normal in the first weeks and months, but he repeated them several years after the fact. Ronald could not accept the truth that his former wife could reject him.

Likewise, with the death of his second wife he frequently protested, "She was so young, just forty-five! It's not fair! We had so much going for us and so much to look forward to." Again, we cannot fault him for expressing such feelings. Virtually anyone else in his shoes would have said the same. But Ronald could not let go.

How have you clung to your losses to the extent that you have denied the inevitability of loss? (For instance, "I bring up the subject of my loss frequently with my friends.")

_____

_____

_____

Dr. Minirth explained, "Ronald, I don't want to deny the very real pain associated with your losses. You need to be honest about your hurt, so in many respects it is good to air your frustrations and your questions. What I *do* want to help you with is in showing you that, though loss cannot be avoided, it does not have to spell defeat for your entire life. You still have good things in your life, and you would be remiss if you lost sight of them."

What about you? Yes, you have been disappointed with painful loss, but what good elements are still in your life? (For instance, "I have other family members who really need me," or "I'm very capable of giving others needed encouragement.")

1. _____
2. _____
3. _____

After several counseling sessions, Ronald admitted, "I guess I need to let go of my shock long enough to realize that I'm not the first person to be disappointed with life nor will I be the last."

He and Dr. Minirth discussed extensively how this did not mean that he would regard his frustration lightly but that he would see it in its proper context. Dr. Minirth gave him an analogy, "If you hold a pebble one inch away from your eyes, it will seem so large that you can see nothing else. But hold it at arm's length and you can see it in perspective with the rest of the surroundings." He explained that his emotional reactions could be managed by keeping them in the perspective of all of his life's capabilities. He did not need to view his loss as the sum total of his life's events.

Use Grief to Rethink Your Priorities

Loss has a way of bringing sober reality into focus in ways other events cannot. In our goal-oriented, drive-to-succeed activities, we can become so engrossed in achievements that we mistakenly allow performances to define our existence. But loss has a way of tapping us on the shoulder with the reminder that relationships, not performances, deserve top billing. It is at times of loss that you can suddenly turn your attention toward inner feelings and long-standing needs, the things that make humans human.

Have you noticed this in your own experience of loss? When it is *you* that is in grief you don't want someone to say: "How are your investments doing in the stock market?" or "Who did you impress today with your achievements?" Instead, you hunger to hear: "I love you and support you," or "Tell me how you've been feeling about all that's going on." You naturally gravitate toward people who can touch you at your point of personal need.

What personal input have you needed as you have struggled with your grief? (For instance, "I need to know that someone understands why I'm so angry and confused.")

_____

_____

_____

What difference would it make for you to know that you are accepted in your full humanness? (For instance, "I'd feel less like an oddity if people were more understanding.")

_____

_____

_____

You may or may not have been fortunate enough to have an ally who genuinely extended permission to be relational, but whether or not you have been blessed in this manner, you certainly know now how necessary it is to put relationships in their place of primary importance. Don't lose sight of this key concept. Initiate deeper relations with those who are in your world.

As Dr. Minirth remarked to Ronald, "Your marriage to Debra was too brief, but I think it made a major impact on you that can lead to significant positive insights. You realized how a loving relationship can awaken a person's spirit. Certainly she did that for you at a time when you had given up hope that you could be successfully connected to someone again."

Nodding as he fondly recalled how he enjoyed very pleasant moments with Debra, he reflected, "Yes, I had just thrown myself into work in earlier years because I had nothing else to turn to. But because of Debra I know that a good life can consist of a lot more than just work and achievement."

"And I can imagine," Dr. Minirth injected, "that in the year since her death you have felt closest to the people who have stepped forward with a deep concern for your emotional well-being." Ronald nodded agreement. The doctor continued, "I'd hate for you to get so far down in your depression that you lose sight of the genuinely good things you have been learning at this stage of your life."

Ronald continued nodding as he pondered the doctor's thoughts. He knew where the conversation was headed, so he said, "I can let my current depression take me back to where I was prior to knowing Debra—living like a machine whose function was to crank out a living and make the fewest mistakes possible. Or I can resolve to continue my willingness to put highest priority on relating, even if it comes with risks."

Because you are feeling depressed in the aftermath of loss, you have probably questioned whether you want to push forward with renewed efforts to keep relationship initiatives alive. That is fully understandable, given the fact that we each need time to regroup when we have been dealt disappointments. But let's assume that a life of perpetual grief and anguish is not what you need. What then is next? Perhaps you will resolve that you can be a success only as you choose to treat people in the encouraging, understanding fashion with which you want to be treated. Notice how this can work:

- A mother whose child has died can determine to be all the more loving to the rest of the people in her life. She realizes that fullness only comes through person-to-person connections.

- A person who has been through the agony of divorce can develop firmer convictions regarding the need for kindness and grace in relationships.

- A wife whose husband has died can befriend other individuals who are experiencing the same predicament.

- A man who has lost his career can focus on building bridges for firmer friendships.

In no way do we mean to detract from the very real reasons you have to feel grieved. We are suggesting, however, that your difficulties can give you a sense of resolve in your life's guiding beliefs.

What positive adjustments could you make that would indicate that your grief has not been experienced in vain? (For instance, "I could choose to be a peacemaker with some of my more tense family members.")

1. _____
2. _____
3. _____

When you have a loss, a piece of your life dies, but not all of your life has to die. Resolve that the balance of your life can still contain fullness and purpose.

Stay in Touch with Routine Matters

A major defining element of depression is withdrawal. Physically, emotionally, socially, you are tempted to take a leave of absence in circumstances in which you might otherwise have been in the spotlight. Because you can legitimately use time out to reflect on your feelings and thoughts, it can be good to pull back from some of your routine when you have experienced a major setback. But you will need to be careful that you do not indulge this practice to a harmful extreme, as is so often the case.

That is what had happened to Ronald after Debra died. When he divorced, he had ceased some of his personal contacts simply because he wanted few reminders of his old life. But when he and Debra married, he renewed his efforts to keep in touch with friends. He was more active socially, he returned to church and renewed involvements there, and he was more visible in community activities. But once Debra's illness became severe, he went back into his protective shell, and a year after her death he had still not come back out.

Has this happened to you? What activities are you now avoiding that you would not have avoided in the past? (For instance, "I've stopped going to my neighborhood social gatherings.")

1. _____
2. _____
3. _____

Why have you decided to withdraw? (For instance, "Other people's lives seem so normal that I just feel like no one would care to know how abnormal I currently feel.")

_____

_____

_____

As time passes, you are only cementing your depression if you remain detached from normal activities. Your withdrawal can represent a form of commitment to a stagnant life. Allow for time to let your sadness play out, but also resolve that you can participate in some of the more routine matters of life.

Admittedly, your depression may not allow you to have the fullest measure of outside involvements, but you do not need to fall to the far extreme of having virtually none. For instance:

- A wife who is trying to make sense of some major disappointments may require extra help from her family in routine chores, yet she can also contribute to household activities as much as she is currently capable.

- A woman who was laid off from a very good job can choose not to hide from her friends even though she feels embarrassment.

- A parent who has suffered major setbacks with a rebellious teenager will determine to keep in touch with other parents.

- A man in a midlife crisis has made some major mistakes and is suffering the repercussions, yet he can decide that now more than ever he needs to keep up contact with family and friends.

A major step forward in Ronald's healing process came when he decided that he could no longer afford to allow his depression to dictate every activity of every day. He confessed to Dr. Minirth, "In the past several months I've turned down offers to get out with others simply because I wanted to stay home and wallow in my bad mood. It got to the point that people gave up on me. Weekends were the worst time because I had no contact with anyone after I left work. I wouldn't share. I let myself gain twenty pounds. I drank pretty heavily. I was really feeling lousy and didn't care if I never woke up once I went to sleep.

"But I've decided I can't go on this way forever," he continued.

"I've realized that I could too easily grow into a crotchety old man, and that's not very appealing."

Ronald then described how he was planning to take better care of himself. It began with a commitment to better personal hygiene and diet. Also, he started looking up old friends, and he took more initiative in keeping contact with his grown daughter. "I'm not back 100 percent but neither am I as far down into my hole as I used to be."

What steps could you take to keep in better touch with routine matters? (For instance, "I could quit hiding behind my telephone answering machine," or "I could make it a point to bring cheer into someone else's life each week.")

1. _____
2. _____
3. _____
4. _____

Keep in mind that we are suggesting balance rather than denial of your feelings. As you engage in activities with others, you do not need to hide the fact that you have been struggling. Most people you know have struggled (or will) with similar problems.

Your grieving process will not be easy, yet your unwillingness to succumb totally to its grip will be another important ingredient in recovering from depression.

7

Finding Release from Control

Step 7. Know that the best way to be in control is to resist the craving to be in control.

When was the last time you went to the zoo? You may have had an enjoyable day, but it's doubtful that the animals felt the same thrill as they watched you watching them. If they were caged, they most likely displayed a flat, disinterested spirit that implied they would rather be anywhere but there.

Let's take this analogy to the human realm (if you don't mind being compared for a moment to animals). When people become depressed, it is very commonly caused by a sense of entrapment, not in the exact manner of a caged animal but in the sense that there are requirements and expectations holding them down, preventing them from openly exploring life as they might under more free, less restrictive circumstances. Depressed people commonly report feeling caged by such circumstances as:

- a marital relationship that consists of heavy-handed, non-accepting demands

- an extended family system that does not allow for much differentness in thought or preference

- a social or church milieu that requires strict adherence to a fixed set of rules

- a work environment that virtually claims ownership of its employees

- friendships that communicate more advice than encouragement

Whether they are conscious of it or not, most people struggle with the temptation to control as much of the surrounding world as possible. Often well-intentioned, people can nonetheless communicate opinions and preferences so strongly that you can feel prohibited from being what you really are. You must fit a mold instead.

Has this ever happened to you? In what circumstances have you felt you had to live more restrictively than you would prefer? (For instance, "My spouse is very stubborn, and I'm expected to just go along with his/her decisions.")

_____

_____

_____

What emotional responses do you feel when you feel controlled by others? (For instance, "I feel very rebellious, like I want to run," or "I feel defeated and unmotivated.")

_____

_____

_____

Allison was one of those people you would never suspect experienced depression. Very pleasant in both her looks and demeanor, she was the kind of person who took it upon herself to be an uplifting presence in the lives of people near her. "I've always had a strong sense of responsibility," she explained to Dr. Carter, "to live according to the Golden Rule. I treat others the way I'd like to be treated. From the time I was young, I had good manners and principles drilled into my mind."

She explained that she had secretly struggled with depression for the past couple of years and that it was becoming so powerful that she was feeling desperate to get away from the circumstances she once enjoyed. For example, she said, "It's gotten to where I can't stand for my phone to ring because it's probably someone who either wants me to participate in some activity I don't want to do or solve some problem I don't want to solve."

Dr. Carter listened carefully as Allison described one incident after another in which she felt compelled to appease someone even if it meant pushing herself beyond her normal limits. For instance, her husband, Brian, was very demanding regarding the way their house should be kept, so what did Allison do? She fretted virtually every day before he came home from work, trying to pick up the mess the kids made and scurrying to prepare the meal he wanted. This was not always easy because her children had busy after-school schedules that required her to set aside her other priorities so she could get them where they needed to be. When she complained or asked Brian for help, he would predictably retort, "I've got my job to do and you've got yours. You're just going to have to buckle under and be more organized. That's the way the real world works!"

As she described her marriage relationship, Allison attempted to put it in the best light possible, but it was clear that she was an unhappy wife. At Dr. Carter's prodding, she confessed, "Brian isn't the screaming type of husband—he's not overbearing in that sense— but he has more expectations of me than he'd be willing to admit. I get *very* tired of having to guess what he wants next, but I always cooperate with him because I never win any arguments when I try to explain to him how demanding he can be."

"I'm hearing you imply that you feel controlled by his moods and expectations," said Dr. Carter.

"Well, you're hearing correctly." Allison's voice was quivering because she was not accustomed to being so open about the tension she carried inside. "I'm afraid to breathe the wrong way for fear that Brian would say something about *that!* He's got more ideas about the way I should conduct my life than I care to know about. I'm very weary of all my obligations, but if I slow down or protest, he'll gripe to the point where it's just not worth it for me to try to buck him."

There is a fine line between living with strong principles and living with strong obligations. One allows for motivation based on choice; the other offers motivation anchored in fear or guilt.

To determine if your environment is too control-based, check the following items that apply to you:

— Other people in my life don't mind telling me how I should handle my responsibilities.

— I'm constantly wondering if I'm going to disappoint or frustrate someone with my decisions.

— Criticism is an all-too-common quality in my world.

— I feel I should keep my feelings in check because they probably don't correspond to others' expectations.

— Duty is a major factor as I consider how I will handle a situation.

— If I admit my weaknesses, I'm probably going to receive advice I don't really want.

— It seems that other people are more interested in my performances than my feelings.

__ Opinionated people annoy me, although I can't seem to avoid them as much as I'd like.

__ Words like *should, must, have to,* and *ought* seem to be ever-present in my vocabulary.

__ I've given up on explaining my needs to others because they probably won't understand anyway.

The more controlled you feel by your outer world, the more emotional turmoil you are likely to experience. If you checked five or more of the above items, you are more likely than most to suffer from depression. Undoubtedly you have conflicting emotions that make you want to shout in defiance but also make you feel shamed for wanting to buck the system. (For greater clarification on this subject, you might read *Imperative People* by Dr. Les Carter [Nashville, TN: Thomas Nelson, 1991].)

What are the strongest evidences in your life that show you are fighting against unwanted control? (For instance, "I'm very defensive with my spouse when problems are discussed," or "People freely tell me what to do.")

_____

_____

_____

How long have you lived in the fear that you would not please your controllers? If you are in a state of depression, it is highly likely that you have been burdened by control problems most of your life. Most of our adult behaviors are extensions of patterns learned in our formative years. You have probably chosen the type of people who surround you because you were predisposed to do so from your early training.

For instance, Allison revealed to Dr. Carter that her early family life consisted of a strong regulatory atmosphere. "My parents were very traditional in their values, and they instilled in me a strong sense of duty to live according to unbending rules. Not that I disagreed with their values, but I had some major conflicts with them because I just felt they didn't allow enough leeway for my own ideas."

"Were they super-strict in discipline?"

"Well, not really. That's what makes it seem odd. They were pretty normal when it came to matters of curfew and things like that. There was this unspoken understanding, though, that I just could not, or better not, do anything to make them feel upset. Dad, in particular, was fairly irritable. He could have his light moments, but he could also get bent out of shape over minor things. I can remember wondering every evening if Dad would be in a good mood or not. Inwardly, I was always checking to determine if I could safely talk to him about the day's events or plans that were upcoming."

Dr. Carter summarized his impressions, "In other words, you felt cautious around your dad to the extent that you had to keep a tight control over your own thoughts and feelings." Allison nodded in agreement.

"Isn't it interesting," he continued, "that you are now married to a man who is also very exacting about his ideas and preferences. I guess when you married you stayed with the familiar."

"I've thought the same thing many times," she said, nodding. "And you know what else? It's not just my dad and my husband who like to control me. Many of my friends are that way too. I attend a church that can be very friendly, and that's where I find much of my social interacting. But I've got to be careful around many of them because they have very strong notions of right and wrong, and I'd never want to be on the wrong side of their opinions."

"What would happen if you were?"

"I'd be on the outs very quickly." Then, shaking her head, Allison admitted, "Over the years I've become one of the insiders in that group. I mean, everyone seems to assume that I think in the same hard-line way as the rest of the group, so I'm looked to as a leader. But frankly it's become a trap I've grown to hate."

As Allison matured throughout her thirties, she felt increasingly alien to her extended family, her husband, her social group. She began seeing them as judgmental and domineering, and she was becoming increasingly troubled in trying to determine how to break free from the entrapments of their expectations and desires.

In earlier chapters we explored the role of suppressed anger and feelings of inadequacy. When you live under a feeling of control, these issues will recur and keep you inclined toward ongoing depression. To have the emotional balance you want, you will need to be released from control by adjusting your interactions with others.

Be Aware of Your Self-Controlling Tendencies

As Dr. Carter discussed with Allison the ways to address her depression, he commented, "You've been explaining how other people seem to control your behaviors and communications, but I'm noticing there is one major person who controls you heavily that you have not yet mentioned."

A puzzled look crossed her face as she asked, "Who?"

Smiling, the doctor replied, "You. In years past you acted out of reaction to everyone else's mandates, but now *you* can be your own worst enemy. Because you've had so much exposure to controlling communication, you bought into the system and began speaking to yourself in very demanding ways."

Allison's nods told Dr. Carter that he had hit the nail on the head. She injected, "I can tell you that I've very deliberately decided that if I can successfully live according to the right agenda then I'll be beyond criticism. Sometimes I'm very hard on myself because it's my way of taking the gun out of the hands of people who might shoot me if I get out of line."

"What are some recent examples of this?"

"Well, I've told you that I'm constantly worried about keeping a clean house for Brian, so I'll often give myself chores to do, even though I hate them and really feel that they could wait. But I've convinced myself that I *have* to be the perfect submissive wife." Her train of thought was in high gear. "And I put similar pressure on myself when I'm with my women friends. This spring I had already decided not to sign up our son for two sports, soccer and baseball. It was too much juggling for me. But some of the other moms were talking with me about providing their kids with early sports training, and, before you know it, I had gone against my best judgment and signed him up for both sports. It's easy for me to say they forced me to do it, but I know in my heart I had buckled to some major self-imposed pressure. I do that kind of thing all the time!"

Allison's depression was her inner signal that was attempting to shout: "Stop! Enough!" She was being pushed by others to fit a mold, and she had made matters worse by pushing herself just as hard as her friends did.

Has this ever happened to you? To determine if you exert too much self-control, check the following statements that apply to you:

— Before I discuss problems with strong-willed people, I decide what I'd better do to keep peace.

— My friends know me as cooperative, but they'd be surprised to learn that I feel taken advantage of.

— It's easier for me to say yes and keep things superficially friendly than it is to say no and create temporary discomfort.

— I have been known to push myself beyond my physical and emotional limits.

— I too quickly accept responsibility for matters that really do not belong to me.

__ When someone else is struggling, my sense of duty to help is stronger than it needs to be.

__ I frequently talk to myself about the way I should act to create favorable impressions.

__ I'm very hard on myself after I have made a mistake or disappointed someone.

__ At times, my sense of right and wrong could be interpreted as rigid.

__ There are times when I act more restrained than I really am.

If you checked five or more, you probably have a strong inner voice that tries too hard to be correct, to the extent of being self-controlling. Keep in mind that responsibility, accountability, and structure are good things to pursue, yet they can be pursued so stringently that you can be more inhibited and emotionally frustrated than necessary.

What are some of the most common ways you overcontrol yourself? (For instance, "I push myself too hard to please people," or "I've held too tightly to the all-work-no-play philosophy.")

_____

_____

_____

Over the years, how has your self-control played into your depression tendencies? (For instance, "I have secretly buried resentments that needed to be openly explored.")

_____

_____

_____

Developing an awareness of unnecessary self-control can be a major step forward in breaking depression's hold. As you realize the potential damage overcontrol creates in your emotions, you can commit to the better alternative: freedom.

Embrace Your Privilege of Freedom

One of the most significant qualities that can carry you toward a fulfilling life is your God-given free will to be whatever you choose to be. Freedom is not a right that you earn nor is it a trait that others can bestow upon you once they deem you fit. Freedom is yours as a by-product of human nature. It is not subject to a vote, nor is it something anyone else can possess for you. Freedom is so much a part of your personality that it can never be permanently removed.

First, let's understand what we are referring to. Far from being a license for irresponsible, loosey-goosey living, freedom can be succinctly defined as the privilege of choices. You have a mind that is capable of ferreting out various options, and in every circumstance you encounter you can determine how you will ultimately respond.

At this point, it is very important to underscore a crucial notion to help you understand why you feel depressed. Though you have possessed freedom ever since you were able to distinguish good choices from bad, others in your life may have so overlooked or disrespected your freedom that your awareness of it has been minimal. You may have had peers or authority figures whose controlling agendas pushed them to ignore your freedom. This caused them to respond to you as if you had no choices, and ultimately it taught you very unhealthy patterns of life.

But does this mean your freedom ceases to exist or that it is improper to exercise? No! It means that other people who are driven by personal insecurities will gladly sidestep truth about human nature in order to satisfy their own preferences. But just because others do not acknowledge your freedom, do not allow yourself to get sucked into defeat or anger or insecurity. For instance:

- A parent may still try to meddle in your decisions well into your adult years, but you are not obligated to give in to unnecessary demands.

- Your husband may motivate you by intimidation, but the truth still stands that you can choose for yourself how to manage your responsibilities.

- Your wife may use false guilt to coerce you into a project, but the decision ultimately belongs to you.

- Friends may attempt to coerce you into a decision by rebutting your different preferences, but you can conclude that it is okay to be different.

- You may feel inclined to argue with extended family about certain family obligations, but you can acknowledge that it is neither your place nor theirs to force compliance.

Old patterns may be hard to break, so if you have a history of succumbing to others' control, you may assume that you are not as free as you really are.

What circumstances have you had in your life that caused you to assume a lack of freedom? (For instance, "My father rarely let me think for myself.")

_____

_____

_____

What conclusions have you falsely held as a result of others' control? (For instance, "I assumed I couldn't trust my good judgment.")

_____

_____

_____

As Allison spoke with Dr. Carter about this concept, she voiced a thought common to many who have been unaccustomed to feeling free. "On one hand I like what you are saying because it sounds so uplifting. When you tell me I can be free it feels like a load of bricks has been lifted off my back." Then her eyebrows turned downward as she asked, "But don't you think this freedom could create some major problems?"

Nodding his head, Dr. Carter replied, "Sure enough, freedom has its risks. What problems did you have in mind?"

Shaking her head as if her mind were on overload, Allison explained, "There are so many things I do now that I'd probably change if I really operated from freedom. There'd be a hundred small adjustments like the way I keep the house or respond to the demands of Brian and the kids. Then there would be some major changes too. I know I would be less driven to keep every one of the burdensome religious mandates Brian wanted me to keep. I would have more of a social life with my friends during the weekdays, even though Brian would resent it because I'd be playing while he is at work. I'm not sure if our marriage could survive me being free!"

Putting her needs in perspective, Dr. Carter replied, "It's a pretty safe bet to say your marriage wouldn't survive years of your depression. Something's got to give because your feelings of enslavement are putting you under."

Realizing, of course, that he did not want to create a monster, Dr. Carter added, "The trait that will keep your freedom in balance is your responsibility. I really mean it when I say you need to feel as free as possible to pursue life in whatever way you deem appropriate, but then that can cause you to think as never before about your ideas of appropriateness. You may decide, as your comments suggest, that freedom accompanied by selfishness would be disastrous. But freedom accompanied by loving desires could be a good combination. What I'm saying is this: It's your privilege, and no one else's, to determine what beliefs will guide you. Just be sure to use your freedom wisely by being responsible with it."

"No one has ever told me that before, ever!" Allison said pensively. "This is going to take some getting used to."

How about you? What changes would happen if you decided to live more freely? (For instance, "I'd spend much less time running my decisions through others," or "I'd take more time to relax.")

1. _____

2. _____

3. _____

Knowing that you can be motivated by selfishness, what risk is there in freedom? (For instance, "I've always wanted to scream obscenities when I'm frustrated," or "Maybe I'd neglect others' legitimate needs.")

_____

_____

_____

When you embrace your freedom, you are doing more than gaining permission to act in whatever way you want. You are also accepting the task of determining for yourself what you really believe. For people who have struggled with depression, this privilege is often a new, scary, exciting experience.

Take a few moments to consider how you have felt restricted or imprisoned by demands (either self-imposed or other-imposed) that you do not agree with. Write down five alternatives that would indicate you have accepted the challenge to be free. (For instance, "I will not feel obliged to call my mother every day like she expects," or "I will give myself permission to have a hobby.")

1. _____
2. _____
3. _____
4. _____
5. _____

By embracing freedom, you may determine to act counter to some of the teachings you have heard from years past. For instance, Allison had learned from her mother (who tended to be overbearing) that she was supposed to just hold in her feelings of frustration if she was to be a good wife to Brian. "After all," her mother had reasoned, "you can't get men to understand things they have no interest in, so why bang your head against a wall?"

In freedom, Allison decided her mother had been wrong and that she could have a healthy marriage even if it meant exposing her frustrations. Her new understanding caused her to rethink many old habits, and she discovered that she was unnecessarily accommodating habits and opinions that were not good for her. She was often in new territory, emotionally and relationally, but she found her freedom to be such a stimulation that it helped lift her from her depression.

Learn to Be Less Guarded

As you accept the reality of your freedom, you may conclude that you no longer have to live as defensively as in the past. Depressed people tend to be very guarded. They have hidden their needs or feelings or perceptions for so long that they are very careful, too careful, about communicating legitimate boundaries. They often rationalize their defensiveness by stating that others will not care if they express their needs, but this is usually a decoy for the fact that they feel awkward about being authentic.

For instance, in her depression, Allison often reasoned that she could not afford to reveal to Brian how hurt she felt when her input was ignored regarding family decisions. "I'd have to spend so much time fending off his challenges that it wouldn't be worth it."

Dr. Carter explained, "You seem to be a very reasonable person who tries to be fair-minded in expressing your needs. Therefore, it makes me wonder why you need to defend your thoughts once you express them."

"Well, maybe I don't feel as confident about my expressions as you seem to feel. I've just always assumed I'd better have good explanations prepared before I present my case. And because I'm not a good debater, I usually keep my mouth shut."

Dr. Carter explained, "Remember, you're a free person. Why defend what needs no defense? If you have a feeling or a perspective to communicate, it's your prerogative and responsibility to let it be known, but it's not your job to defend it or to sell it. Let your thoughts stand on their own."

Do you ever defend when it really is not necessary? To get an idea of your tendencies, check the items that could apply to you:

— I tend to be intimidated by strongly opinionated people, so I back down in discussions with them.

— Often if someone disagrees with my views, I am thinking of my rebuttal as that person speaks.

— I feel I'd better have a good explanation for the way I think or believe.

__ I play into others' guilt trips even when I'm not guilty of anything.

__ I tend to be cautious in the way I disclose my feelings to others.

__ I'm constantly wondering how I could have expressed my thoughts more appropriately or accurately.

__ I feel that I have to work hard just to be taken seriously.

__ When others become stubborn, I dig in and become stubborn too.

If you checked four or more items, you may be so worried about defending yourself that you have lost your ability to be who you are. It's not necessary to work so hard to force others to understand you or agree with you. The more you defend, the more you get caught in problematic emotions that feed depression.

What defenses do you most commonly exhibit that keep you feeling controlled? (For instance, "I feel I have to explain my financial maneuverings to my father," or "I'm always afraid someone will judge me if I expose beliefs that are not mainstream.")

1. _____

2. _____

3. _____

As you keep your defenses up, what happens to your depression? (For instance, "I feel defeated in my hopes that my family will really understand my needs.")

_____

_____

_____

By dropping your guard, you would be making a commitment to authenticity, which is defined as letting your outward life be a consistent reflection of your inner thoughts. Authenticity is a central ingredient to freedom and to a healthy life. Without it emotions become twisted, but with it you are more likely to keep a cleaner emotional slate.

Whether you realize it or not, other people receive cues from you, telling them how they should respond to you. If you expend extra energy defending your perceptions or if you are very closed and hesitant to assert a position, others will assume that you are insecure and will treat you as a less than equal person. If, however, you communicate without heavy defense and you exhibit a calm confidence, you can quietly invite others to think well of you.

What do you project to people? Based on the amount of defensiveness you exhibit, what conclusions might others draw about you? (For instance, "They probably think I'm wishy-washy," or "I've been told that I come across as arrogant and unapproachable.")

_____

_____

_____

Let's look at some examples of how a commitment to freedom could allow persons to be less rigid or tense in their responses to others:

- A husband is unreasonably nitpicky with his wife regarding the way she manages her time. She decides that since her choices are responsible she need not waste her time convincing her spouse that she is really an okay person.

- A child whines and questions a discipline decision the parent has made. Knowing a defense will only escalate the tension, the parent calmly replies (as often as needed): "Nonetheless, that's the decision I've made."

• A boss at work is very critical, but the employee decides that it is better to go about business as responsibly as possible without worrying about having to appease his erratic moods.

• A member of someone's extended family constantly criticizes other family members. That person could choose to argue with the critic or pacify him, but she determines the best response is to just be herself.

As a free person, you are not required to perpetually look over your shoulder worrying about how you are going to satisfy others' control needs. To do so only keeps you vulnerable to harmful emotions since it is a complete impossibility to read others' minds in order to adjust accordingly.

What are several common incidences in which you would benefit by laying down your need to defend yourself? (For instance, "When my spouse tries to invalidate my opinions, I'll sidestep the temptation to justify the way I think.")

_____

_____

_____

What changes in your self-perception would be apparent as you projected more freedom and less defensiveness? (For instance, "I'd start seeing myself as a more credible person," or "I'd feel less need to win others' approval.")

_____

_____

_____

See the Value of Accountability

When you elect to live freely, you take a major step forward in your battle against depression. Accepting freedom implies that you believe enough in yourself that you will not timidly allow others to play god. Instead, you can search out *the* God to determine what you understand His will to be for your life. Your sense of direction in life can acquire deeper roots.

But let's be careful not to carry freedom to a point of selfishness or irresponsibility, as could be the case. Because humans will always be interconnected, relying on each other for love and encouragement and stimulation, we need to make room for commitments. A spirit of cooperation and loyalty can keep freedom from being abused, and it can keep you on track in those relationships that count the most.

In the days of Roman rule, a slave owner could give his slave papers of release, declaring him completely free. But sometimes a freedman would arrange to work for the former owner in a slavelike capacity but with the understanding that it was done with no compulsion or coercion. This person then became known as a bond slave.

What relationships would function best if you maintained a bond slave's attitude? For instance, you may decide that your marriage is not perfect, yet you can freely decide to have the highest sense of dedication to your spouse. Or perhaps your employer is not someone you would choose to be close friends with, yet you can give a full effort to your job every day.

Where would you benefit most from the bond slave's mind-set?

_____

_____

_____

What commitments would you make even if you knew you were free to choose otherwise? (For instance, "I would commit to love my spouse who does not have the same capacity to love me as strongly," or "I could hang in there with my teenager, knowing the relationship seems one-sided right now.")

_____

_____

_____

As Allison contemplated how she might act more freely in her reactions to Brian's controlling style, she admitted, "I don't want to rip our marriage apart. Brian can be frustrating, but we also have some good moments together. I don't want him to think I'm some sort of ungrateful, demanding wife who refuses to consider his preferences or needs."

Nodding agreement, Dr. Carter said, "Marriages don't have to be perfect in order to be satisfying. I think it's wise to allow for some errors or differentness rather than hoping one day you can be completely rid of all your tensions."

"I still *want* to love Brian and to be cooperative. I'm realizing that I need to relieve some of our tensions by jumping through fewer of his hoops, but I also still intend to be there for him as his wife."

Wisely, Allison was not confusing freedom with license to act as rudely as she wanted. She had determined not to live under ridiculous control requirements, but her bond slave's mind-set caused her to still respect commitments.

In your life, how might you exercise commitment and freedom at the same time? (For instance, "Though I wouldn't have to come running every time my mother calls, I would still keep in touch with her legitimate needs.")

_____

_____

_____

As you understand how to respond to the control demands from others, make room for the fact that some controllers may feel unsettled for a while. Yet, cling to the awareness that your commitment to live confidently is better than ten arguments in which you ask others to agree with your choice of freedom. Let your appropriate life speak where words cannot.

8

Accepting Ugly Reality

Step 8. Make allowances for painful truths.

By now it is clear that depression is usually an emotional response to very undesirable circumstances. Pain, rejection, loss, maltreatment, control, neglect. These are the factors that can cause you to collapse under feelings of despair, anger, bewilderment, and isolation.

It is probably safe to say that there was once a time in your life when you dared to hope you would not be burdened by such aggravations. For instance, teenagers who have known pain and confusion hope for the day they can find freedom from their oppressive situations. Likewise, most married couples tie the knot with the hope that this will be the relationship that alleviates their vulnerability to loneliness. Virtually no parent brings a child into the world with anything but eager anticipation that that child will live a happy and productive life. Daring to hope, you can formulate highly motivating ideals that may also become disillusioning.

It is a hard truth to accommodate, but virtually every life will contain pain that seems unfair or untimely. Each person has flaws, insensitivities, blind spots, chronic weaknesses that cannot be completely erased. This is true of yourself and of every person you have contact with. The curse of the sin nature on mankind ensures that any interaction involving humans can break down or disappoint. Though not a pleasant thought, it is reality nonetheless.

Those who make room for human error, even gross errors, will be less likely to suffer emotional damage since their mental preparedness will keep them from feeling completely shocked when the letdown occurs. Those who do not make room for human error will be strong candidates for depression.

Are you prepared to accept ugly reality? As you consider the concept of accepting unwanted intrusions, what initial hesitation crosses your mind? (For instance, "I can accept imperfection, but not when it is as severe as I have known," or "I hate the idea that unfairness exists.")

_____

_____

_____

_____

Family Histories and Pain

Do not feel alarmed if you have difficulty with the problem of pain. We all do. In our practices we have discovered that if you come from one of two types of family histories, though, the concept of pain will be more difficult to digest. Perhaps you had (1) the "ideal" upbringing or (2) the chaotic upbringing. Let's look at each.

The Ideal Upbringing

When Charlotte spoke with Dr. Minirth she was clearly straining to keep up a pleasant front. Smiling graciously as she spoke, her outer demeanor was inconsistent with the depression she was describing. Her original complaint was feelings of extreme overload caused by her many stresses. Her two grade-school daughters were more rambunctious than she could handle. Her husband was a well-respected businessman, but she felt unfulfilled because he was involved in too many activities that did not include her. She was active in several community functions but was finding them to be more burdensome than she had bargained for. Her symptoms showed a clear pattern of depression: easy crying, sluggishness, excessive need for sleep, weight loss, poor concentration, chronic edginess.

When Dr. Minirth asked Charlotte if she had any history of similar problems, she defensively said, "Oh, no. No, I've never had problems like this before. I came from the most wonderful family you could want. We were always known for being very close, and we still are. I know there's no such thing as perfection, but my parents were as close to it as you could get." She almost seemed insulted that Dr. Minirth would assume there might be a problem there.

"Tell me what the communications were like in your original home."

"Well, Mother was the type who was always available. My sister and I couldn't wait to get home from school because she always had a snack, and she would set aside whatever she was doing to tend to our needs." She went on to explain that her mother had been and continued to be her best friend. Theirs was the house the other kids gravitated to because it was full of warmth and encouragement. "Dad wasn't as involved in our lives as Mother, but he was easygoing and supported us in whatever we wanted to do."

Charlotte spoke in such glowing terms about her family that she

143

could not bring herself to say anything negative about her past. "Really, I know you may not believe me, but my childhood was ideal. We could search for days, but you'll not find any skeletons in my childhood closet."

Her adult life with her husband and children was a different story, however. Her husband, Bill, was in a sales position that kept him gone from home a lot. She had always dreamed of the idyllic marriage with a sensitive and supportive husband; instead she found Bill to be disinterested in her feelings and too tired to want to participate enthusiastically with family matters. Her daughters, ages eight and eleven, fought chronically. Unlike her own experiences with her mother, Charlotte found the bond with her girls to be lacking. Rather than appreciating her efforts to be Mother of the Year, they preferred she leave them alone to be with friends.

Trying to explain why she felt depressed, Charlotte cried, "Nothing in my adult life is the way it's supposed to be. Why can't anyone understand that I really do have lots of love to give? Why won't anyone cooperate?"

Have you ever felt that way? Some people have a vision of the wonderful life instilled in them during their formative years, and they enter adulthood hoping to continue living sheltered from the strains and quirks that face most people. For instance, Charlotte had *some* reason to feel disappointed because it is normal to desire pleasant camaraderie with primary family members. Her depression, though, was caused by her unpreparedness to accommodate routine breakdowns or incompatibilities. During her time of counseling with Dr. Minirth, she was never able to say anything worse about her original family than that they might sometimes have been preoccupied or modestly irritable. She genuinely believed they were virtual saints—just as it should be.

To determine if you have an overidealized dream of what life can give you, check the following statements that could apply to you:

__ I can become nervous or upset even when disagreements are relatively minor.

__ Others have accused me of holding on to a "knight in shining armor" dream.

__ It is very important to me that relational problems be settled as soon as possible.

__ I've been taught that if a family could just love each other enough, it would eliminate the possibility of emotional problems.

__ My view of my past could be described as flowery.

__ I have had a very strong need to keep my parents as proud of me now as they were in the past.

__ I have had a best friend relationship with one of my parents.

__ We didn't really confront each other in my home of origin, mainly because it just wasn't necessary to do so.

__ In my early home life we accentuated the positives, not the negatives.

__ Others used to express envy regarding the wonderful way my family would get along.

It is good to have positive past experiences to draw upon, so do not assume we are skeptical of positive reports about your history. Too much idealism, though, can set you up for a harsh fall when your adult experiences cannot maintain the lofty standards established in that wonderful past. If you checked five or more items, there may be a very real need for you to redirect your thinking about the normalcy of suffering. You don't want your positive experiences to create in you the assumption that you cannot tolerate anything less than wonderful.

What experiences in your past may have caused you to be ill-prepared for some of the pains in your present? (For instance, "My parents never argued," or "We never really had to talk about conflicts.")

1. _____
2. _____
3. _____

The Chaotic Upbringing

Some people have very troubling stories to tell about their early family life. Abuse, fighting, and neglect were the norm for many depressed adults, and they recall early fantasies of being rescued from their ongoing miseries.

Kirk explained to Dr. Carter that he survived a chaotic childhood by fantasizing how his adult life was going to be almost the complete opposite of his childhood. His father had been very stern, to the point of being unapproachable. Kirk and his siblings never knew when their dad might blow his stack, but it was often enough that they made deliberate efforts to avoid him. His mother, though not possessing an explosive temper, was equally offensive. Very bossy, she had opinions on every subject and was prone to emotional flare-ups, usually crying, when someone disagreed with her.

As he recalled his past, he explained, "The only way I could keep my sanity was to become occupied somewhere away from home. As a grade-school boy I'd try to get away to a friend's house as often as possible, and during my teen years I'd work as many hours as my employer would allow. I hated my family life. At eighteen I joined the Navy and never looked back. Now, I only see my family at major events, and then it's for as brief a time as possible."

Kirk's fall into depression came in his early forties because of a job downturn and family stress. He was paid on a commission basis, and his company hit hard times. He spent a couple of years struggling financially. His wife, Wanda, had never been close to him, and their emotional distance had increased with his job pressure. His face looking haggard and hopeless, Kirk said, "How long am I going to have to suffer because of people and circumstances out of my control? I had enough problems in my childhood to last a lifetime, and now it seems that my current circumstances are just too much. It feels like God keeps piling on misery after misery. Where's it going to stop?"

Have you ever felt that way? What situations have caused you to feel like you have had more than your fair share of personal problems? (For instance, "My father was never very gentle; now I'm stuck with a husband who doesn't know the first thing about responding to a woman.")

_____

_____

_____

When you feel depressed, what kind of "I wish" statements commonly run through your mind? (For instance, "I wish we'd never have money problems again," or "I wish *someone* would figure out how to love me.")

1. _____
2. _____
3. _____

Common Myths About Depression

Whether your past was idealized, as in the case of Charlotte, or chaotic, as in Kirk's situation, you can easily fantasize how you can and should have a worry-free adult life, but such unrealistic expectations will only make you more inclined to be depressed. Though it is not wrong to have hopes and dreams, your need for positive input may feel so strong that you become bitterly disappointed and disillusioned when you have repeated encounters with tensions you had hoped would never visit you again.

To avoid depression's trap, you will need to make room for some realities that admittedly are not what you want to hear but are true nonetheless. This means you will need to set aside some of the myths common to people with depression. Let's examine some of the major myths.

Myth: "If I live right I can avoid pain."

In very different ways, both Charlotte and Kirk illustrate how a dream for pain-free living can be at the root of depression. Charlotte, with her privileged history, was protected from real struggles by parents who mistakenly assumed they were being loving through their overindulgence when in reality they were encouraging an attitude that eventually became the foundation for manipulative maneuvering. "When my struggles begin to create tension," she would inwardly reason, "all I have to do is complain the right way and someone will make it all disappear." Sure enough, her parents would oblige her, and she could move on happy as a lark.

But where did that leave her as an adult? She still had problems, in fact more complex ones than before, but no parent to bail her out. So what did she do? She became demanding—of her husband, toward her children. She clung to the illusion that pain could somehow be circumvented. If she lived right, she assumed, the world would fall conveniently into place and she would be free from stress.

For instance, one evening Charlotte's husband came home and found her crying in the bedroom. "The kids have been awful today," she said. "I try and I try to be sweet to them but they still pick at each other, and they don't show me any respect. They're not even teenagers yet, but I'm already looking forward to the day they leave home. They can't even appreciate the fact that their mother loves them dearly and would do anything to make their lives wonderful."

Do you see how Charlotte was clinging to an idealized assumption that if she lived correctly (which she tried to do), her girls would respond wonderfully (which they often did not do)?

In what circumstances do you fall into the same painful misassumptions? (For instance, "If I live consistently within my religious guidelines, surely I will be blessed with a trouble-free life.")

_____

_____

_____

What is the error in your assumptions? (For instance, "Deep down I know God doesn't promise painlessness.")

_____

_____

_____

Kirk was caught in a similar mind-set, but he approached it from a different angle. Having been exposed to anger and neglect all his childhood, he had decided that the way out of his hole was to be a model citizen. Finding his wife to be unsupportive during a time of financial crisis, he had seen his feelings of disillusionment with people grow to enormous proportions.

Speaking about this with Dr. Carter, he said, "When I was a kid I basically had to write my family off. They just weren't there for me, so I learned to expect nothing from them. But that wasn't supposed to happen with Wanda. Look what I've done for her through the years. She's gone back to work within the past year because we need the money, but for years she didn't have to work at all. Doesn't that count for something? Plus, I've never been the insensitive husband or father. I may not be the best communicator in the world, but at least I try. Where is she when I need her most?"

Kirk's disillusionment, like Charlotte's, was fed by the attitude: "I've held up my end of the deal, what about you?"

What are some similar disillusionments you have experienced? (For instance, "I can be everyone else's shoulder to cry on, but no one really lets me be human.")

_____

_____

_____

Neither Charlotte nor Kirk was entirely wrong in having the desires that fed depression. Being interdependent by design, humans naturally hope when they perform right it will create a more favorable environment. As Kirk said, "I've always thought if I scratched your back, you'd scratch mine."

But let's look at an ugly truth: Emotional pain can exist even when it seems it should have been duly alleviated. You can act appropriately, commit to honor and integrity, live conservatively—and yet be afflicted with pain. Why? Your world is imperfect. In theological terminology, it is infested with sin. It is a certainty that any person can be capable of insensitivity, anger, rudeness, unawareness. Even people who are generally well-intentioned can show such flaws. This has always been true, and until the end of time as we know it, it will remain true.

In spite of such dreary truth, you need not despair. Pain exists, but so does hope. For every problem you may encounter, there is a coping skill. You may not solve the problem of pain, but you can apply healthy personality traits to a degree that they carry you through your affliction. For instance:

• An adult whose parent has died tragically can determine to reflect on that parent's positive traits, becoming all the more committed to show those healthy qualities to others.

- Someone who has been stricken by major disease or physical duress can learn to show genuine appreciation for those in a helping capacity. Relationship skills can increase.

- If you have experienced serious marital problems, you can affirm the value of encouraging communication, and even though you do not receive encouragement as you would like, you can be a bright spot for others.

Accepting the reality of painful truth does not require that you just collapse and give in to it. (Remember earlier chapters focusing on stating needs and setting boundaries.) But it does mean that you will view painful truth in the context of all of your other positive skills.

Write down some of the painful truths you have had a hard time accepting. (For instance, "I have ongoing health problems," or "I can't deal with our long-standing family disputes.")

1. _____
2. _____
3. _____
4. _____

What behavior or attitude adjustments might you make that would indicate that you accept the reality of your pain? (For instance, "I could become less of a critic and more of an encourager," or "I'd become more disciplined in activities I know would help me.")

1. _____
2. _____
3. _____
4. _____

Right living does not create immunity from your problems, so make room for the reality of unwanted intrusions. Yet, hold firm to your right living because with it you find integrity and hope.

Myth: "Surely people will accept and understand me."

When you experience depression you look for people who will understand and support you. But how do you respond when it does not happen, or when it does not come from the desired source? Most people experience one of two problems: 1) They try to force closeness that will not come, or 2) they sink further into their miseries because acceptance seems so elusive.

It was this myth that sent Kirk into an emotional tailspin. He told Dr. Carter, "I was able to live with the fact that my parents didn't know how to love me because I knew they were products of their own difficult pasts, and besides I didn't have a choice regarding the fact that I was in their family. I just learned to bide my time until I could leave home.

"But the problems with my wife have really gotten to me. I chose her and she chose me, so I've always assumed it meant we had a deeper type of commitment, but apparently she thinks otherwise because she's just not very open to me. And to make matters worse, I really feel I have to be guarded in telling friends about my marital problems because they don't want to be bothered by that kind of thing."

Was Kirk wrong in wanting a deeper level of understanding from his wife and friends? Not at all. Yet he was faced with the harsh reality that these people either did not want to expend the effort to connect with him or were not aware of the best way to do so. Has this ever happened to you?

When have you felt most in need of acceptance and understanding? (For instance, "Several months after my son died, people assumed I'd be over my grief," or "Recovering from past abuse has been more tedious than most people can understand.")

1. _____

   _____

2. _____

   _____

When you hope against reality that you will be fully understood, you become a prime candidate for the emotion of loneliness, a major factor in depression.

Check the following items that apply to you so you can determine how powerful a hold loneliness has on you:

__ At times I feel as though I do not belong to the group I am with.

__ Though I want to share my feelings with others, I have given up because it will probably do no good.

__ I get the feeling that I am much more willing to help others than they are to help me.

__ I just don't trust people like I used to.

__ Sometimes it seems easier just to get away by myself; I don't want to be hassled by people anymore.

__ I've been accused of being aloof or withdrawn, but really I'm just hesitant to show how hurt I really am.

__ When I am with others I can develop uncomfortable anxiety symptoms.

__ I often wonder why people can be so easily insensitive.

__ Even if I told my problems to others they probably wouldn't know how to respond.

__ I entertain fantasies of how nice it would be to have more comfortable surroundings.

If you checked five or more, you are probably experiencing loneliness and could have difficulty accommodating the fact that you may experience similar disconnected feelings in the future.

If you have felt emotionally misunderstood, you have probably had more unsolicited advice than you need. For instance, if you tell a friend about a major disappointment with your son, you are likely to receive advice like: "If I were you, I'd . . ." or "Have you tried doing . . ." Most of the advice is well-intentioned; nonetheless, it shows how uncomfortable people can be with your humanness. If a solution can be found quickly, they would be freed to move on to friendlier subjects.

What experiences have you had of sharing deep emotions only to have solutions thrown back at you? (For instance, "Whenever I try to tell my spouse about a parenting problem, I'm told how to handle it better," or "If I discuss the extent of my grief with a friend, I'm told that better days are just ahead.")

1. _____

_____

2. _____

_____

During times of pain you want understanding, yet many people are not equipped to give it. Afraid of their own emotions, reluctant to get too involved, people will sidestep the possibility of discussing the real you, leaving you feeling isolated or misunderstood.

This was a particularly difficult problem for Kirk. He told Dr. Carter, "You're the only person in my life who seems willing to understand my gut-level feelings. I'm grateful for it, but it also makes me wonder why others just won't make the effort to know the real me."

He and Dr. Carter decided that he needed to make allowance for the fact that some people in his life would never catch on to what he wanted. But then the doctor suggested, "Surely there is someone in your life who would make an effort to know you more deeply if they only knew how to do so."

Kirk nodded. "I have a friend at the office who's been through counseling, and he's aware of my circumstances. We haven't talked extensively about my emotions because I haven't sought him out for that purpose, but I think he'd be open."

"You'll need to capitalize on that. Explain to him that you're not looking so much for advice as you are looking for understanding. It won't solve the problem of all the other people in your life who don't know how to help you in your emotional need, but it can keep you from feeling completely isolated."

Simply put, not all people in your life want to take the time and effort to understand your unique needs. But you need not collapse in hopelessness; there are *some* people who will genuinely do whatever it takes to connect with you. It can be your task to make yourself available to those people so your isolation will not seem so permanent.

Once you find the right persons who would want to relate closely to you, you may need to explain your special needs clearly. For instance, Kirk spoke to his friend at work and told him it would be most helpful if they could meet weekly for the purpose of sharing and talking about personal issues. He explained that he didn't need advice as much as a good listening ear. The friend was enthusiastic to accommodate this request because he too desired a more authentic relationship.

Who could you choose to confide in? What might you tell that person about your special needs? (For instance, "I have a friend at church who's always been an encouraging type. I'd like to let

155

him/her in on my secret that I'm struggling in ways few people know.")

_____

_____

_____

_____

Don't assume that the lack of understanding shown by some is representative of the way all people are. Take the initiative. Even as you accept the reality of some loneliness, search for those whose main priority is to relate.

Myth: "Contentment comes from external sources."

In the past couple of decades, the psychological world has been flooded with information addressing the importance of a spiritually based sense of security. Some of the information, frankly, has been misguided because it humanistically encourages people to worship self or some mystical deity. Some information, though, has been right on target as it emphasizes a personal commitment to the sovereign God who has made provisions for us through the redemptive work of Jesus Christ. In our dealings with depressed people, we have discovered that many people publicly portray themselves as God-believing, spiritual beings, yet when crunch time comes, they revert to the wish that they could be rescued by more satisfactory external circumstances.

That was certainly the case with Charlotte. She told Dr. Minirth that she had been strongly indoctrinated in the Christian faith as a child and continued to practice her religion as an adult. "My faith in God is as strong now as it ever was," she told him.

A puzzled look crossed Dr. Minirth's face. "I've heard you state several times how important your faith is, but as I get to know you better I'm learning that you've placed such heavy requirements on your family to be your salvation that your Christian faith has lost its comforting power."

Fidgeting in her chair, she said, "Well, what am I supposed to do, ask God over for dinner and get Him to wake up my husband and straighten out my kids?" She was clearly angry. "How's my faith supposed to make my problems disappear all of a sudden?"

Have you ever felt this way? When have you set your spiritual focus aside in order to attempt to find comfort in your external world? (For instance, "When I get emotionally wiped out, I want a stiff drink," or "I love God, but I'm wanting even more for my family to love me.")

_____

_____

_____

_____

Dr. Minirth explained, "A fundamental mistake you are making is in insisting that your outer world must conform to your specifications so you can then get on with a comfortable relationship with God. But it doesn't work that way. Perhaps in your childhood you were fortunate enough to have a family that made God's love seem very real. You will need to recognize that God's love, His direction, continues to be real today even if your current family members do not give you what you want. Don't let others dictate whether or not you will live in the strength that can come from your spiritual life."

Perhaps you are aware of the biblical concept of being "content in whatever state I am" (see Phil. 4:11). Though not explicitly stated, there is a very real implication that circumstances will disappoint, yet God's strength can be found. Several examples of this concept can be found:

- You are distraught because of the death of a close friend. Without denying the depth of your hurt, you can find an ability to be loving and encouraging toward family and friends.

- You are reeling in shock after learning of a spouse's infidelity, yet you can hold on to the very real truth that you still have worth even in the face of your mate's rejection.

- You have been devastated by rejection from a group, yet you eventually realize how such an experience will prepare you to respond kindly to people you know who have had similar experiences.

- You are struggling with seemingly endless physical ailments, yet you choose to focus on the small daily successes that can bring moments of joy.

As you consider how you could put your spiritual strength more specifically into play, what circumstances come to mind? (For instance, "In spite of my family tensions, I know I can still live within the healthy personality traits that are godly.")

_____

_____

_____

Myth: "I can get rid of my depression forever."

This myth is difficult for depressed people to dispel. The alternative is to admit that you may struggle again with depression, a prospect you are not likely to endorse enthusiastically.

Allow us to underscore the strong belief that depression does not have to be terminally oppressive. We believe that you can adjust habits and patterns that can greatly reduce your inclination to feel depressed. People who have consistently applied insights regarding their emotional and thinking patterns have found that they can experience victories for years and years.

Yet, the truth remains that you can still be susceptible to depression because you are not immune to ongoing potentials for rejection, illness, death, and so forth. Consider the analogy of a man who has undergone knee surgery. The knee can be successfully repaired to the point of normal functioning, yet that man will need to be a little more cautious than most because he knows the susceptibility is there for future damage. He does not have to feel defeated by this reality, only careful to monitor his bodily movements.

In the same way, do not feel threatened by your susceptibility to depression. Given the right circumstances, anyone could experience this problem. Permit yourself to be human even as you commit to practicing solid coping skills. Rather than giving yourself the mandate never to be depressed again, make it your goal to be in an ongoing process of daily monitoring your emotional and relational habits for the purpose of being as balanced as you can be *today*.

At first, Charlotte protested when Dr. Minirth suggested that she lay aside her lofty demand that she should not have to suffer with depression, but her feelings eased when he explained his reasoning. "When you put pressure on your life to be perfect, a paradoxical effect occurs. You can try so hard to be above problems that they overwhelm you. But on the other hand, when you are not overwhelmed by the possibility of having your emotions, they won't hit you with such a vengeance."

Showing new awareness, she replied, "From my childhood years, I was taught to assume that I should be exempt from the struggles of common people. Our family was unique, meaning it was problem-free. It's been hard for me to swallow, but I'm coming to terms with the fact that I was not allowed to have a full view of my humanity. I need to accept more completely life's imperfections even as I continue to learn how to live with the least amount of distress."

Kirk also had to draw a similar conclusion, though he did so from a different angle. Because of his troubled past, he had falsely built a hope that he could shield himself from pain with the right adult moves. Realizing he couldn't, he had to choose either to allow himself to collapse emotionally or to restructure his hopes toward a more realistic expectations level. Choosing the latter meant making allowance for unwanted stress, but as he put it, "If I know that I am still capable of letdowns, I can know more clearly how to gear myself so it won't be so dreadful."

If you made a clear allowance for the potential of depression, how could this *help* you in the future? (For instance, "I'd learn to expect less and therefore be disappointed less regarding my extended family.")

_____

_____

_____

Perspective. Balance. Reality. As you learn to stay away from false positive myths you will be less inclined toward disillusionments and simultaneously you will be less inclined toward the extreme emotions on the negative side of the ledger.

9

How Personality Styles Affect Depression

Step 9. Understand how your personality can predispose you to depressive feelings.

"Is it true that some people have a more natural inclination toward depression than others?" This is one of the most common questions we hear when counseling individuals through their difficulties. Many people live with great frustration because they observe how others seem to bounce through life with little or no real emotional damage coming upon them. "Maybe I'm just a weak person," they reason. "Apparently those other people have something going for them that I don't have."

When depressed people fall into this form of self-put-down we quickly encourage them by putting their emotional struggles into a much broader perspective. As we have already shown, many circumstances can influence the direction of people's emotions, as can exposure to varying patterns of emotional and communicational management. No two people can be expected to have the same disposition because we each have such unique experiences with the outer world.

But let's take our perspective even further. Each individual has an inborn personality type that functions as a filtering system, interpreting events and relationships, telling the person how to respond. Your personality type, coupled with your many life experiences, can predispose you to emotional reactions differing greatly from the reactions you see in others. In order successfully to address your depression, then, you will need to know your personality tendencies. There are some elements within your personality you can learn to strengthen, some you will need to minimize.

How well do you know yourself? Though it would be impossible for us to give a full discussion regarding all personality types, we will examine six of the most common personality patterns we see in depressed people, helping you identify their strengths and weaknesses, showing you how persons within those types can take specific steps to avoid pitfalls that could keep depression going. As you survey the information in this chapter, understand that you will probably see yourself in more than one category. Your uniqueness lies in the combination of personality styles. You can take suggestions then from each category as you continue to formulate a special game plan for monitoring your depression.

The Dependent Personality

People with a dependent personality have a core desire to please. They usually have a pleasant demeanor and a true servant's heart. Friendly and loyal, they do not mind taking on menial tasks, nor do they mind playing second fiddle to more dominant people. They usually have a reliable and cooperative spirit, and they pride themselves in their ability to avoid controversy. If anything, they work too hard to keep peace.

Problems arise for people of this persuasion because they often find themselves feeling either dominated or burned out. Because of their giving spirit they have a hard time saying no, meaning they can easily feel stretched too far in commitments or obligations. Underlying their loyalty can be struggles with fear and guilt, prompting them to push dutifully to keep others happy, sometimes to the point of tolerating abuse or great discomfort. Taking onto themselves the responsibility for others' actions, they too easily feel badly about themselves when others do wrong.

Do you recognize any dependent personality traits within yourself? To check your inclination in this direction, mark the following items that apply to you on a consistent basis:

— I tend to take care of other people's problems to the extent that I get wrapped up in them.

— When others tell me what to do, my natural inclination is to try to please them.

— Experiences of rejection strongly affect my feelings of self-worth.

— I have been known to rescue people from their problems, even if it would probably be better to let those persons struggle on their own.

— I would rather let other people do the confronting.

— I would rather listen to other people talking about their problems than reveal my own.

— When a close friend is too busy to talk to me I wonder if I have done something to offend that person.

— Somehow troubled people seem to find their way to me.

— I really don't mind taking on lowly jobs that others might not care to do.

— I have been known to give to the point that it hurts. Others see this as an opportunity to manipulate me.

How did you do? If you responded to six or more of these items, you probably have strong leanings toward the dependent personality style. You have such an overriding desire to be cooperative or compliant that you allow your preferences to be too easily defined by others.

Whether you fully consider yourself as a dependent personality type, try to think of some incidences when your desire to do good has gotten you into trouble. What comes to mind? (For instance, "My kids know if they plead strongly enough I'll give in to their demands," or "I still act compliant when I'm with my mother.")

1. _____
2. _____
3. _____

When people of this personality persuasion are regularly associated with friendly, supportive family and friends, they rarely struggle with depression. Their tendency toward pleasant servitude keeps them buoyed. But when they are attached to insensitive or dominant or manipulative people, depression is very common. Because they naturally tend to hang in there with others' demands, they make the mistake of giving too much of the benefit of the doubt. This means they will usually endure problems far beyond what most other people would. For example, a dependent wife may make excuses for her temperamental husband as he treats her insensitively. Or a loyal worker may remain in a nowhere job because he or she does not want to let fellow employees down by looking for work elsewhere. In these types of situations, dependent people will suppress their needs and emotions, taking depression upon themselves while fiercely (and perhaps unwisely) clinging to their loyal commitments.

If you find yourself operating from dependent personality traits, a major adjustment could be made that would keep you from your depression. You could communicate boundaries much more firmly and in doing so you would send the message to others that you want them to respect you, just as you respect yourself.

For instance, the wife who tolerates insensitivity from her husband can choose not to jump every time he barks out a demand. She can have a life that includes independent preferences or feelings even as she continues to keep her commitment to be a responsible wife. Likewise, the worker who works too hard to keep the nice-guy image can more clearly enunciate to his fellow employees what he can and cannot do for them. He can see the value in not always taking on someone else's problems.

How about you? What adjustments could you make in your life-style to communicate firm boundaries more clearly? (For instance, "When I tell my kids they will experience consequences for misbehavior, I'll actually follow through," or "I won't feel compelled to go along with a friend's suggestion just as a means of appeasing that person.")

1. _____

_____

2. _____

_____

What fear will you have to overcome as you choose to act more firmly? (For instance, "I can't continue living in fear that my father will cut me out of his will if I make good independent decisions," or "I'm not going to buckle under the fear of being labeled as impossible or rebellious.")

_____

_____

_____

Your depression will ease in direct proportion to your understanding that it is both good and responsible at times to be your own separate and distinct person.

The Obsessive-Compulsive Personality

Consider the two words *obsession* and *compulsion*. An obsession is a repetitive thought pattern. A compulsion is a need to act on an idea. An obsessive-compulsive personality is distinguished by repetitive, almost unstoppable thought patterns that lead to a powerful need to carry a task to full completion. Obsessive-compulsives tend to perform according to a strong sense of duty and obligation. Uncomfortable with change, they can often be inflexible and hardheaded. Their need for order causes them constantly to pursue solutions to whatever problems may arise. They strongly dislike loose ends.

In the best light, people of this personality persuasion are usually well-organized and methodical. They use logic well (in fact, they *insist* on doing things logically), meaning they can be counted on to bring order to disarray. With a heavy emphasis on performance, they are usually high achievers, and they find their self-esteem in the completion of projects. They often appear strong and decisive and together, but the flip side is that they will usually try to hide feelings of uncertainty and insecurity.

To determine if you have leanings toward the obsessive-compulsive personality, check the following items that commonly apply to you:
— When faced with disorder or glitches in my schedule, I struggle with annoyance or impatience.
— I am a person of decision and have a hard time tolerating wishy-washy situations.
— When I tell someone I'll take care of a job, it's as good as done.
— If a project is left unfinished, my mind keeps wandering back to it until it can be finished.
— I have been known to voice criticisms too easily, or I give advice too freely.

166

— Other people might describe me as black-and-white in my thinking.

— Often I'm so focused on a task I don't want to take time out to attend to someone's feelings.

— I like lists.

— My preference is to have things neat and in their place.

— Sometimes I feel pulled between obedience and defiance. I like putting things in order, but I don't want others telling me how to do it.

Did you recognize any familiar traits in the list? If you checked six or more items, you probably have consistent tendencies toward obsessive-compulsive thinking. On one hand, you can be an asset to others because of your precision; on the other hand, you may struggle with your emotions frequently because the world does not readily fit your mold.

What are some common circumstances in your life that draw out your obsessive-compulsive tendencies? (For instance, "I cannot tolerate clutter in the kitchen," or "When someone displays a hurt or vulnerable emotion, I feel compelled to fix it or provide solutions.")

1. _____

2. _____

3. _____

A major downfall of obsessive-compulsives that makes them vulnerable to depression is their inability to make room for emotions. For example, one man complained that his wife was very expressive, both in her feelings of excitement and of frustration. Each time she would expose herself in this way, he would respond with something like: "What is *wrong* with you?" or "I just don't know why you have to react like that." Often the wife was well within normalcy in her feelings and impressions, but she was not within *his* norms. The husband felt his role to be the corrector, but when he failed to pull his wife into his mode of thinking he would feel distraught and hopeless. "Apparently she doesn't love me" would be his conclusion. His need for order and logic caused him to interpret differentness wrongly as rejection.

Obsessive-compulsive people struggle most with anger ("Why won't you do what I say?") and guilt ("What could I have done differently to solve this problem?"). Because they work too hard to place subjective emotional experiences into objective measurable schemes, they can eventually conclude that life is a miserable rat race full of people who just will not be cooperative.

To reduce the vulnerability toward depression, these persons need to take a much less stringent view of their performance criteria. Yes, achievement and performance are good, but emotions and perceptions cannot, will not, be easily crammed into a formula. Acceptance of diversity in thought and reaction needs to be incorporated into their interactions with others. For instance, the husband who tries to force his wife to handle the kids exactly as he would, needs to let her have more leeway in feeling what she feels and behaving as she behaves. The worker who drives himself to achieve excellence needs to learn that it is okay to leave work on the desk in order to take time out to relate to the feelings of friends and families.

As you consider how to be less driven by obsessions and compulsions, what adjustments would you make? (For instance, "When my spouse expresses emotion, I could refrain from advice-giving and show an interest in the personal things being said," or "Maybe I don't have to clean the kitchen today.")

1. _____
2. _____
3. _____

Obsessive-compulsives bring emotional duress upon themselves because they deny the truth that the world is not all black-and-white. They also miss the fact that life consists of much more than achievement. When they learn to live with loose ends, taking time out to share and to accept emotions and unique perceptions, they will take a major step away from depression and toward calm composure.

The Histrionic Personality

As strongly as the obsessive-compulsive is driven by the need to perform, the histrionic (or hysterical) personality is driven by emotional expressiveness. When sharing their feelings, which they often do, they can appear dramatic and excitable. It is common for these people to exaggerate and use superlatives, meaning they can experience wonderful highs and awful lows. They are very people-oriented and feed off of the emotions of others, either to the positive or negative direction.

Because of their expressive, emotional natures, histrionic personalities are often charming and socially adept, making wonderful friendships while putting people at ease. They have a natural willingness to discuss personal matters and can quickly focus on underlying feelings and needs.

Because of the inclination to relate on an emotional, personal level, these people can also be easily upset when emotional attention is not received. They have a powerful need to be emotionally affirmed, and when they do not receive satisfactory attention they too easily assume feelings of rejection or despair.

To determine if you exhibit traits consistent with the histrionic personality, check the items that consistently describe you:
— I have been known to overstate my emotions when trying to make a point.

__ I can laugh easily and cry just as easily.

__ Not only am I not uncomfortable with groups of people, I enjoy the social arena.

__ I have a strong desire to receive love and to give it away.

__ It is hard for me to keep my feelings inside for a very long time.

__ Most people would say I add color to my surroundings.

__ I like to do things that are exciting and thrilling.

__ I have been known to display mood swings that sometimes baffle others.

__ Some people might think I am flirtatious when in fact I'm just being friendly.

__ I like doing things spontaneously rather than having to be tied to an agenda.

If you checked six or more items, you probably have strong leanings toward the histrionic personality style. Your emotions lead the way, meaning you are vulnerable in unfriendly or rigid circumstances.

When do you see your histrionic traits most readily on display? (For instance, "I really look forward to the sharing times I spend with my friends," or "I tend to respond emotionally in family disagreements.")

1. _____

2. _____

3. _____

What negative side effects have you noticed that accompany your emotional displays? (For instance, "Sometimes my emotions are so strong, people do not hear my logic," or "I get tied up in knots when people can't relate to my feelings.")

1. _____

2. _____

3. _____

Being so people-oriented, histrionics fear rejection to the extent that experiences of misunderstanding or invalidation send them into an emotional tailspin. Their desire to feel emotionally connected is both good and normal, but in its exaggerated form it can lead to anxiety and tension. This, then, becomes the foundation for depressive experiences.

For instance, one woman legitimately lamented how her husband was stubborn in making any effort to relax and enjoy relations with his in-laws. He was a quiet man who did not understand the need for open displays of affection, nor did he make much effort to notice his family's needs for the purpose of becoming an encourager. This wife's histrionic tendencies caused her to beg and plead with him to be more friendly, and the more he resisted her suggestions, the more distraught she became. She eventually became very depressed because she felt very rejected by him while also feeling chronically tense because he would not relate with her family as openly as she would like.

Like this woman, perhaps you too have had experiences of getting so caught up in legitimate emotional reactions that those emotions eventually mushroom and take over your personality.

Describe a recent situation in which this has happened to you. (For instance, "When my son refused to obey me recently, I began crying strongly, feeling like I was an unfit parent.")

To keep your histrionic tendencies from working against you, it would be in your best interest to lower your expectations that others can or will understand your emotional needs. Don't succumb to the tendency to place your emotional stability into the hands of imperfect people. No human can be expected to know your feelings through and through, nor can anyone affirm you so consistently that you will never have to fear feeling isolated again. Make allowance for the fact that your emotions and perceptions are unique, and therefore not always the same as everyone else's.

List some situations in which you could lessen your emotional reactions by being less expectant of others. (For instance, "I won't be surprised if my spouse does not share the same enthusiasm about a phone call I received from a distant friend," or "I'll not overreact when someone expresses dislike for one of my preferences.")

1. _____
2. _____
3. _____

As you learn to anticipate the potential for different emotional styles, you will not register as much shock or disappointment when things run counter to your preferences. You may need to train yourself to speak a little less excitedly or to use fewer superlatives. Let some logic guide you, especially when you know your feelings would like to take over.

What differences would you notice if you applied more thought and less impulsive emotion to your circumstances? (For instance, "I'd be less shocked by my brother's anger," or "I would react less to my spouse's irritations and try to figure out what he/she is really trying to say.")

_____
_____
_____

Your biggest challenge will be to have enough inner composure that you will not give in to the tendency to let emotions pull you into exaggerated reactions.

The Avoidant Personality

Some people seem to live with the goal of sidestepping as much personal involvement and vulnerability as possible. Uncomfortable with personal disclosures or emotional attachments, they perpetually seek to maintain a ruffle-free comfort zone. They are willing to give up moments of great excitement as long as it also ensures they will be free from great stress. Staying away from hassles or inconveniences is a major goal. These people have what might be described as an avoidant personality.

Not all people of this personality persuasion would be described as dull or drab, as you might presume. Often, avoidant personalities can be pleasant and friendly, seemingly kind or caring, but as you come to know them deeper you will find such traits to be superficial. They are kind or friendly *as long as* there is little personal cost to them in terms of emotional investment. They will relate with others only after they are convinced that acceptance will be safely given and with few demands.

Avoidant persons tend to handle conflicts with finely tuned passive aggression. Not the type to initiate loud or boisterous displays of anger, they reveal their hidden frustrations through traits like evasiveness, halfhearted commitments, procrastination, indecisiveness, and unaccountability. Though on the surface they can seem cooperative, beneath the surface is a quiet stubborn streak that causes them to rebel against the suggestion that they should invest greater efforts into maintaining deeper emotional ties.

To determine if you ever exhibit avoidant tendencies check the items that often apply to you:
— Others might describe me as pleasant yet hard to get to know.
— I'd rather deal with my problems privately than air them out in the open.

__ I can go long periods of time feeling frustrated without letting others know what is going on inside.

__ I resist being tied down to promises or commitments. I am a "maybe" or "could be" person.

__ There are times when I'll just leave people hanging regarding decisions I might make.

__ Sometimes when others are sharing personal issues I may quietly be tuning them out.

__ I can let problems linger rather than taking initiative to figure them out.

__ There have been times when I have indulged secret sins others still do not know about.

__ When asked how I'm doing, I'll typically answer "okay" even when I'm miserable inside.

__ People might be surprised to know how often I disagree with what they feel or believe.

How did you do? If you responded to six or more of the items, you probably have a strong inclination toward the avoidant personality style. Your methods of managing emotions lean so much in the evasive direction that you often will have many loose ends that eventually will cause frustrations to pile up.

When are you most inclined to exhibit avoidant traits? (For instance, "I'm friendly with my wife as long as she keeps discussions upbeat, but I look for the way out if she expresses hurt or anger.")

_____

_____

_____

What has been the effect of avoidant behaviors on your closest relationships? (For instance, "I find myself not wanting to mess with certain family members because they've always got problems.")

_____

_____

_____

Avoidant personalities generally dig themselves into holes of depression because they miscalculate their need for relational involvement. After years of not engaging others with deep emotional ties they can find themselves feeling lonely and isolated, especially if a trauma visits them. For instance, one man spent years plodding innocently through marriage, being a good provider but ignoring virtually all his wife's emotional needs. When she filed documents for divorce, she shouted, "I've been trying for years to get your love and affection, but you never cared!" Once she left he had virtually no one to turn to because the relationships he had formed through the years had been quite shallow, and besides, he did not know how to express his emotional needs. It was at this point that he became depressed, feeling that he had had all the props kicked out from under him.

To be less susceptible to depression, if you have avoidant leanings you would serve yourself well by taking the risks involved in letting others know who you are. Expose your hurts. Empathize with others as they expose theirs. Stop worrying so much about keeping relationships light and airy and show a willingness to grapple with conflict. Hear others' confrontations and develop specific step-by-step plans to remedy your deficiencies.

What changes could you make to stop avoiding tough personal issues? (For instance, "When someone asks how I feel I'd say, 'I'm struggling,' then explain myself," or "I'd make it my goal to show keen interest in others' feelings.")

1. _____
2. _____
3. _____

Specifically, where would you need to take initiative most? (For instance, "I'd get real with my brother who has been at odds with me for years.")

_____

_____

_____

Your greatest obstacle in overcoming avoidant tendencies will be the foreign feeling you will experience as you reveal your real self. You will want to run at that point, or at least redirect your effort toward friendlier subjects. To avert this, tell a trusted friend in advance that you have a tendency to duck personal vulnerability and ask that person to help keep you accountable.

The Narcissistic Personality

Ancient Greek mythology gives us the story of a young man named Narcissus who leaned over the edge of a pond to refresh himself and fell in love with the image he saw in the water. He then spent his life in pursuit of that person (himself) he so deeply adored. From that story we get the term *narcissism*. Narcissistic personalities have an excessive admiration of themselves to the point of self-absorption. They are in constant pursuit of a life that will bring pleasure and ease, and they reject the notion that they might have to struggle for happiness. They have a difficult time relating to others' feelings because they invariably will draw a conversation back onto their favorite subjects. For instance, if a friend relates an incidence involving a recent illness, the narcissist will predictably say, "Oh, that reminds me of a time when I . . ."

While these people can often seem charming and extroverted, they have a hard time maintaining lasting, satisfying relationships. When commitment to a relationship is required, when acceptance of imperfection is needed, they either cease their relational efforts or complain strongly. They dislike having to live outside their own comfort zones. Understanding this, you could recognize that even the friendly gestures of a narcissist might be suspect. They are friendly—as long as there is a payoff for being that way.

To determine if you might have narcissistic tendencies, check the following items that would apply to you:
— Looking good and maintaining a favorable image is important to me.
— At social gatherings I can "shoot the breeze" with anyone, yet privately I avoid deep discussions.
— I prefer to stay away from people who have preferences or lifestyle habits that differ significantly from mine.
— I have a history of great highs and lows in my romantic relationships.
— People who have made money and exude power impress me.
— I can respond angrily or defensively when my preferences or opinions are questioned.
— It is not unusual for me to have many acquaintances but no real confidant.
— I can be demanding of those closest to me.
— I like for others to know about my achievements and successes.
— I often indulge dreams of great success or ideal love.

Did you notice yourself in any of these items? If you checked six or more, you probably have a strong leaning toward narcissism. Be aware that most narcissists hesitate to admit their self-absorbed tendencies because they, by definition, want to present themselves in the best light. So if you think you might have leanings in this direction (and you want to change), let someone who knows you well respond to the above items on your behalf. Be open to objective feedback.

Narcissists are readily vulnerable to depression since life cannot and will not cater to their every craving. They believe the world owes them favored treatment and are genuinely surprised when it does not come. For instance, an engaged man was surprised when his fiancée became angry after learning he continued dating another woman. "But we're not married yet," he protested. "Why make such a big deal about it?" He became despondent and sought counseling when she broke off the engagement. However, the counseling did not have a very strong effect in his life because he soon found another girlfriend and pronounced his depression cured.

This man's depressive experience is very typical of a narcissist. His feelings collapsed not because he had been unfairly injured but because he could not have it all.

Can you think of a similar episode of depression that resulted from limits you did not want? (For instance, "I can't tolerate having to give up social events because of my children's needs.")

_____

_____

_____

If narcissism is something you struggle with, you will remain inclined to emotional highs or lows until you realize you are not the center of your universe. The world does not owe you the favored treatment you think you deserve. You can and will be required to use self-restraint.

How could you do a better job of taking self off center stage? (For instance, "I can devote more time to my spouse's preferences," or

"There is no need to feel slighted when others don't share my enthusiasm for a night out on the town.")

Narcissists will be less depression-prone only when they truly understand the happiness that can come from serving others even when it means self's pursuits are not fully accomplished.

The Borderline Personality

Some people can create a first impression that shows them to be normal and friendly, but as you get to know them more deeply you realize they seem incomplete. When life presents no problems, they are just like everyone else, but with difficulties they seem to fall apart. Moodiness, erratic emotions, clinging behaviors, strong anger—these are traits common to the borderline personality. The term *borderline* implies they seem to teeter on the brink of breakdown. You never know when they will emotionally erupt.

A strong identifying trait of borderline personalities is the fear of being alone. They have a strong need for stimulation, are bored quickly, and are easily led astray. Their need for personal connections will often cause them to compromise well-taught principles, leading to impulsive and self-destructive behaviors such as alcohol abuse, sexual promiscuity, wasteful spending, and binge eating. It seems they will do whatever the immediate crowd wants them to do as long as they can be assured of attention.

The borderline's volatile relational patterns indicate a strong identity confusion. You might say they suffer from a disintegrated self-image. They often have instability in relationships or work because they do not know themselves well enough to know what they really want. They typically latch on enthusiastically to a person or a project;

then weeks or months later they will shift gears and look anxiously for something new to stimulate them. They may not know what that something else is, but they want it anyway.

To determine if you might have borderline personality traits, respond to the following items:

___ I have a history of broken relationships.

___ Boredom comes easily to me. I need lots of stimulation.

___ Spending time by myself is very unnatural for me. I need to be around people.

___ I have had numerous experiences with alcohol abuse, sexual involvements, partying.

___ If I get involved in conservative living (church, for example) I lose interest and go to something more exciting.

___ If it appears someone may reject me, I can become vindictive and erratic.

___ Once I develop an interest in someone, I latch on quickly and strongly.

___ When I feel discouraged, I think and sometimes speak about dying.

___ I'm not above using strong threats or accusations if it will help me get my way.

___ I have sought help for my problems several times, but it hasn't really done much good.

If you checked six or more items, you may have strong leanings toward the borderline personality. It would be a good idea to seek help from a qualified counselor so you can develop an understanding of the neediness and desperation that drives you. A word of encouragement: Stay with the counseling even when it causes discomfort. Don't run.

Borderline personalities commonly complain of depression. Because they have a history of clinging to others in times of need, they have not fully developed their own internal sense of competence. Usually, they have been trained to feel secure by means of personal beauty or social smoothness or athletic achievement, things that do not really have deep staying power. When they cannot solve their problems through charm or when others fail to be their emotional cushion, depression hits.

In addition, borderlines usually have low levels of trust. Perhaps abusive situations created a lack of trust or perhaps shallow love with parents caused poor feelings of attachment. This creates a conflict; they dearly want closeness, but simultaneously they fear it.

In your history, what tendencies have you had that demonstrate a desperate need to be lifted by others from your feelings of desperation? (For instance, "In the midst of marital tension, I have looked for outside nurturing," or "Rather than being alone I'd rather go to a bar, or even just a movie, so I can be around people.")

1. _____
2. _____
3. _____

To overcome your tendency toward depression, you will need to cease your desperate search for a human savior and learn to draw strength from within. This will require serious, sometimes slow soul-searching that will not feel normal. Your need for immediate gratification will need to be set aside as you learn to find peace in simpler matters of life. For instance, instead of having to phone a friend right after having an argument with your spouse, you would serve your needs better to set aside an hour for quiet reflection, pondering how you could handle your tensions more calmly.

What specific circumstances can you think of in which you could give a slower, less panicked response? (For instance, "When my weekend plans are canceled at the last minute, I won't *have* to scramble to find new plans," or "When a friend disappoints me, it's not necessary to tell others immediately about how unfairly I've been treated.")

1. _____

2. _____

3. _____

Learn to rely less on others. Do not give in right away to your self-serving impulses. Take time to contemplate your beliefs; make sure they are your own, not borrowed from parents or friends. If you have strong borderline leanings, seek professional counseling, and don't bolt when the counselor suggests something you do not want to hear.

Your Unique Personality

As you look back upon the six personality descriptions in this chapter, understand there are many more personality types we could have mentioned, but these tend to be the most common we encounter in cases of depression. Our point here is not to pigeonhole you into one type but to provoke you to realize that your inborn temperament can have much influence on the form and severity of your depression.

You have probably noticed that your personality does not fit neatly into just one category. This does not mean you are schizophrenic; it only means your personality is a unique blend of traits and tendencies that cannot be duplicated by anyone else.

A good way to prioritize your efforts in overcoming your depression is to determine the strength of certain personality tendencies in comparison to one another. For example, you may guesstimate that your personality is driven this way: 10 percent narcissistic, 40 percent histrionic, 35 percent dependent, 15 percent obsessive-compulsive. There are certain insights about each personality type that can guide your efforts, some insights carrying more importance than others.

Though you cannot be exact or scientific, estimate the percentage of influence each of the six personalities plays in your life:
— dependent personality
— obsessive-compulsive personality
— histrionic personality
— avoidant personality
— narcissistic personality
— borderline personality

Based on your awareness of your unique personality tendencies, what priorities do you have as you seek to be more emotionally balanced? (For instance, "I need to be less perfectionistic, more accepting," or "I want to cling to others less and develop my own inner direction for life.")

1. _____
2. _____
3. _____

Awareness is half the battle. By being tuned in to your personality tendencies, and by drawing awareness from the previous chapters, you can be well on your way to more stable emotions.

10

Evaluate Your Medical Needs

Step 10. Be open-minded as you consider the medical aspects of depression.

Depression is rarely the result of just one contributing cause. Many factors underlie your experiences of depression, as we have seen in the preceding chapters. One cause that you should carefully examine is the biochemical aspect of depression. Your biological makeup and emotional makeup have strong interconnections, meaning difficulty in one area can trigger problems in the other. Everyone has patterns of social, emotional, developmental, genetic, and physiological factors that influence the susceptibility to depression. When one factor is off course, it is very likely to throw the others out of balance as well.

Consider a very simple analogy. Suppose you have spent an entire day pushing yourself through a very strenuous exercise regimen. By evening you feel weary as your body reminds you that you are not

185

as young and fit as you would like to be. At that moment, how capable would you feel to tackle a major family dispute? If you are like most, you will think, "Please, not now. I'd like to be of help, but at this point I'm too worn out!"

When you have endured repeated stresses and strains over months and years, your body can become fatigued, losing its effectiveness in sustaining its own internal checks and balances. The result is that your emotions will function poorly in situations that might otherwise be routine. Because unresolved negative emotions have an energized quality, depressed people find that they have been drained of their ability to "get up and go" as they should. They tire easily, sleep poorly, think erratically. Something internal (physical) is very wrong, and it needs to be addressed.

Strong evidence supports the fact that many depressed people can find relief through the proper use of antidepressant medicines, which correct biochemical malfunctions as people go through the process of resolving social and emotional strains. In spite of the success of medical interventions, though, some people remain resistant when it is suggested they consider their use. One such person was Richard.

"I've never been the kind of person to take medicines," Richard told Dr. Minirth. "Even when I have a headache or a cold I'd rather just let it run its course. My wife tells me I'm stubborn, but I'd prefer not to get hooked on any pills. I can't understand why you're asking me to take antidepressants."

"First, let me assure you that I appreciate your conservative approach toward medicines," Dr. Minirth replied. "There is no need to introduce a substance into your system unless it is truly warranted. In your case, the evidence seems to indicate strongly a need for a medical approach."

Richard had told Dr. Minirth that he had been experiencing depressed feelings for over a year. His wife had suffered a stroke about eighteen months before and was still not up to speed physically. He had two grown sons living out of town and a daughter about to finish high school when it happened. Suddenly, his world was turned upside down because his wife, Annette, had been such a good home-maker that he easily took her for granted. The daughter helped where she could, mostly in household chores, but she was very active with friends and with a part-time job, so she couldn't do it all. Richard was a supervisor on an assembly line and could not get away from his responsibilities, so his life was on overload because he had so much to do when he got home from work each evening.

"I don't like complaining or telling people about all my problems," he often said. So for months he carried the burden of his wife's illness and his extra responsibilities alone. During this time he became much more irritable than normal. He regularly felt despondent, as if the weight of the world was on his shoulders, but no one else knew or cared. He would go to sleep each night around 10:30, but by 2:00 A.M. he would awaken and remain wide awake until time to get up. Nothing seemed to correct this sleep disturbance. Going against his grain, he had succumbed to taking over-the-counter drugs to help his sleep, but the pattern remained.

Feeling isolated from friends, he chose to stay secluded, rationalizing that he didn't have the time or energy to socialize anyway. When family members offered to help with Annette's care, he refused, not because he didn't need it but because he didn't want to show vulnerability or weakness.

"I'm worn out," he told Dr. Minirth on their first visit. "I *did* talk to a minister at my church about my feelings, and he was really kind, but no matter what people might say to encourage me, I still feel down, and I'm not sure there is any way out, at least not until Annette fully recovers."

Dr. Minirth knew that Richard could lessen his inclination toward depression by adjusting his patterns of emotional management. For instance, on several visits they discussed how he was doing himself no favors by refusing help. Playing the hero role only caused him to become bitter because secretly he resented his wife's neediness and

187

the extra work required of him. They discussed ways to diminish his bitterness by being more assertive with his extended family and being more honest about his grief. This helped, but even after making adjustments, his depressed symptoms persisted.

Dr. Minirth explained, "When you are under unusual stress for prolonged periods of time, your body may not function as properly as you would like. In a weakened emotional state you can experience physiological breakdowns that will not go away. That's when you could make good use of antidepressant medicines. They can help you recover so you can feel more useful and productive. In fact, in many cases a person *won't* move forward until attention is correctly given to the medical aspects of depression."

What about you? Have you experienced ongoing symptoms of depression that would not go away even after making good adjustments in thought and behavior? What symptoms persist? (For instance, "I can't stop crying spells when they come.")

1. _____
2. _____
3. _____

We have mentioned numerous signs and indicators of depression, but certain ones tend to indicate problems involving biological factors: erratic sleep patterns (either interrupted sleep or excessive need for it), easy inclination toward crying, ongoing pessimism and moodiness, significant change in weight, decreased sex drive, low energy, poor concentration, decreased motivation, and thoughts of suicide.

Which of these symptoms are ongoing in your life and how long have they persisted? (For instance, "Sleep disturbances, over six months," or "Unusual moodiness for at least a year.")

1. _____
2. _____
3. _____

A medical doctor, preferably one very familiar with psychiatric medicines, can help you recognize trends indicating the need for medical intervention. Do not hesitate to consult a doctor immediately.

What Are the Common Antidepressant Medicines?

It can be difficult to explain the workings of antidepressant medicines chiefly because the exact action of drugs within your chemical structure is not fully known. We do know a great deal, though. All of your thoughts and feelings, both pleasant and unpleasant, are the result of many electrochemical reactions occurring throughout your body and the brain. Internalized stress results in the release of "fight or flight" hormones from the adrenal gland. Primary among them are epinephrine, norepinephrine, and serotonin. As stress continues, this system apparently continues to release these hormones until they are depleted.

The eventual decrease in the level of these hormones can influence the body in many ways. A depressed person can develop endocrine disturbances that result in the symptoms of depression, as well as other symptoms such as rapid heartbeat, nervous stomach, and increased vulnerability to colds and upper respiratory infections.

When your symptoms of depression persists for weeks and months, this indicates that your emotional stressors are so entrenched that your body is paying the toll. You will need to adjust your manner of responding to emotions and circumstances, and you may need the introduction of medicines for several months to correct the biochemical malfunctions caused by the stress.

In general, four main classes of antidepressant medicines can be identified:

First-Generation Antidepressant Medicines: Tricyclics

Imipramine was the first tricyclic antidepressant developed in the late 1950s, and it set the stage for several other drugs that act upon the body in very similar ways. Included in this group are amitriptyline (Elavil, Endep), nortriptyline (Pamelor, Aventyl), desipramine (Norpramine, Pertofrane), doxepin (Sinequan, Adopin), protriptyline (Vivactil), and trimipramine maleate (Surmontil). These medicines are very similar in their effect on the nervous system in correcting the biochemical imbalances. The selection of one drug over the other is generally based on the potential of side effects such as blurred vision, dizziness, or weight gain.

Second-Generation Antidepressants: Heterocyclics

The medicines in the heterocyclics category work in generally the same fashion as the tricyclics but were developed to include fewer or less severe side effects. They include such drugs as amoxipine (Asendin), maprotiline (Ludiomil), and traxodone (Desyrel).

Third-Generation Antidepressants: Bicyclics

These still newer medicines have become quite popular because of the much lower incidences of side effects. Chief among these drugs are fluoxetine (Prozac) and the unicyclic compound bupropion (Wellbutrin). Perhaps you have read or heard reports about side effects of Prozac. If these reports concern you, consult with a doctor who has extensive experience with this medicine. Our experience with Prozac has been favorable, requiring the same caution we would use with any of the other antidepressants.

MAO Inhibitors

Where tricyclics and other medicines increase the amount of essential neurotransmitters in the brain, Monoamine Oxidase (MOA) Inhibitors aid in treating depression by slowing the breakdown of neurotransmitters. These medicines have been around for years, having been discovered in the 1950s in the treatment of tuberculosis. Included in this group are phenelzine (Nardil), tranylcypromine (Parnate), and nialamide (Niamid). These drugs are most often used in treating depression accompanied by hysteria, phobia, or anxiety. Because of the common side effects of increased blood pressure and weight gain, these drugs are generally used only when medicines in one of the first three groups prove ineffective.

How Are the Medicines Administered?

Antidepressant medicines are not taken in the same fashion as cold medicines or pain relievers, which are used only upon the presentation of symptoms. Antidepressants work cumulatively over longer periods of time and must be taken steadily each day in order to create the right effect within the body. Usually, the dosage of antidepressants is begun relatively low and then gradually built up, with the dose increased about every three or four days until the desired dose is attained. Depending on the medicine, a depressed person may require two to six weeks on the drug before receiving a full therapeutic response. Then, the medication is usually prescribed for six months or longer, depending on the person's reactions and adjustments to the circumstances involved in the depression. When improvement is adequate, the patient will be able to taper off the medicine in the same time increments as it was begun. Most will not experience an immediate relapse of symptoms.

Some people find that they return to depressive symptoms shortly after ceasing the medical intervention. This can be because of ongoing unresolved tension or genetic inclinations that predispose that person to be vulnerable to depressive symptoms. We have seen the need in some of these cases to maintain the person on low doses of the antidepressant for as long as the symptoms require it. Careful monitoring by a physician, of course, should always accompany long-term use of medicines, but you should not interpret the need for medicine as a sign of personal weakness. Instead, be thankful that chemists and physiologists have unraveled enough of the body's mysteries to determine how to hold such symptoms in check.

Are Antianxiety Medicines Used in Depression?

Very often people who experience depression also have accompanying anxiety. The telling symptoms include feelings of uncertainty, muscular tension, trembling or shaking, restlessness, worry, and inability to relax. Anxiety can also be shown in physical complaints such as dizziness, headaches, upset stomach, frequent urination, diarrhea, and high pulse rate. When people experience an "anxiety attack," they can have symptoms that feel like a heart attack: tightness in the chest, strained breathing, numbness in the arms.

Patients who describe anxiety symptoms alongside depressive symptoms often find relief when they begin taking antidepressant medication. But sometimes an antianxiety agent is additionally needed to ease those symptoms. Great care must be taken because some medicines of this nature have a potential of addiction if taken for long periods of time at high doses. Moderate use usually does not result in addiction, so you can feel comfortable in their use as long as you monitor it carefully with your doctor.

The key difference between antidepressant and antianxiety medicines is that the latter provides short-term relief for its symptoms, whereas the former works cumulatively and requires time before showing an effect. Commonly known as "tranquilizers," antianxiety medicines relieve the physical tension in your muscular system. Librium and Valium were among the first used in this country for the treatment of anxiety, but they are not as popular now because of the introduction of newer, safer medicines.

Other medicines used in treating anxiety include Tranzene, Ativan, Serax, and Xanax. Antihistamines have also shown some helpfulness in treating anxiety. They include Atarox, Vistaril, Benadryl, and Nortec. A newer medicine, Buspar, may take a bit longer for the antianxiety effects to be evident, but it is not thought to be habit-forming and can be effective when taken regularly for long periods of time.

A group of medicines developed for the treatment of various cardiac and blood pressure conditions can also be used in certain anxiety-related cases. Medicines such as Catapres and Inderal have been prescribed in recent years for prevention of migraine headaches and panic disorders, as well as in assisting the withdrawal symptoms from opiates.

Another category of anxiety-reducing medicines includes sedatives, drugs used primarily as sleeping pills. Used for short-term relief of insomnia (which is a common symptom of anxiety), these medicines include Dalmane, Restoril, and Halcion. Long-term use of these agents is not recommended since they can produce a physiological dependence.

Finally, a medicine that is not strictly a sedative, Antabuse, is sometimes used in the treatment of alcoholism. When a person has difficulty withdrawing from alcohol or has poor impulse control, Antabuse is given daily, usually in the morning, and will produce a strongly distasteful reaction if alcohol is introduced within twenty-four hours. The reaction includes vomiting, sweating, rapid pulse, rapid respiration, and skin flushing. Some consider it a controversial treatment, so it is generally used only with individuals who are sincere in wanting to stop drinking or who have good intentions but very poor follow-through.

What Treatment Is Best for Manic-Depression Symptoms?

A unique type of disorder may require a different approach from those used for clinical depression. Manic-depressive illness, also known as bipolar disorder, usually requires the use of a drug called Lithium.

Manic-depressive illness is characterized by wide, disabling mood swings. Some people can be susceptible to it (depending on levels of stress and biological predisposition) their entire adult lives. Some may experience one or a few episodes, with it never reappearing.

Three categories of bipolar disorder are possible:

Bipolar, Manic Type

Bipolar, manic type, is typified by mania, a condition during which the person's mood changes from its normal state to an extremely overactive state. During a manic state, the individual usually cannot sleep, talks very rapidly, exhibits enormous outbursts of energy, is easily irritable and impatient, and has racing thoughts. Usually, the mania leads to poor and impulsive decisions, often with serious financial, occupational, social, and even legal repercussions. Sometimes the symptoms can be so severe that the manic person is completely delusional or paranoid.

As an example, one manic person stayed up all night typing letters on his computer to about fifty people (including the state's governor, the president, and his corporation's CEO). The next day he emptied

194

the family savings to invest in new stocks and bonds. Finally, he became completely delusional, thinking he was one of the twelve apostles.

In most instances, the manic patient requires hospitalization for the purpose of starting medical intervention. The behavior is usually so "off the wall" that it cannot be initially treated in an outpatient setting because of the high likelihood of future unpredictable behaviors. Hospitalization is a place where the manic behavior can be more readily contained until the medicine effectively relieves the symptoms.

Bipolar, Depressive Type

Some people have phases of depression that predictably occur at fairly frequent intervals (for instance, once every autumn for four months). They may never experience classic mania symptoms, but there seems to be enough of a rhythmic cycling in emotion to warrant the bipolar diagnosis. These individuals are likely to experience the same depression symptoms mentioned elsewhere in this book and will probably have a difficult time doing routine daily activities or going to work. During these times, suicidal thoughts can be prominent.

A very high percentage of these people have already tried the other antidepressant medicines, finding some or little relief. The administration of Lithium can be made with the assumption that it can affect the biochemical deficiencies more accurately than the traditional antidepressants.

As an example, we treated a woman recently who would experience depression every autumn as regular as clockwork. During the late spring and summer she would feel normal energy and engage in a very active lifestyle. But each October or November a deep depression would overcome her, rendering her useless. She would spend hours in bed during the daytime. She became moody and pessimistic, and this trend would continue for about three or four months, after which she would slowly come back to life.

Having run through just about every known antidepressant, she was given Lithium and found immediate relief. Because she had never had manic episodes, it had been easy to overlook the potential of a bipolar disorder. But the predictability of her downswings each year indicated to us that she was bipolar, depressive type.

Bipolar Disorder, Mixed

Some people have recurrent problems with both mania and depression. These changing symptoms can alternate every few days or over a period of months. Typically, such people will experience the flurry of the impulsive manic behavior followed by severe feelings of sadness, regret, or remorse. During the depression episodes, pleas for help will be expressed, and it is at that time that individuals will most willingly receive help.

For instance, a man who sought treatment reported great swings in mood and energy levels. For a period of three or four weeks he would be extremely successful in his sales job. Exhibiting tremendous enthusiasm, he couldn't wait for each day to begin because he just knew he would be able to close sales at a record pace, which he did. But mysteriously, he would then experience several weeks of demotivation, wanting to sleep constantly, feeling apathetic about any and all responsibilities. He was greatly relieved to learn that his problem was not lack of motivation but a treatable condition. With the introduction of Lithium, his lifestyle smoothed out as he ceased both the overactive and underactive swings.

An important aspect to know about Lithium is that it is not a *cure* for bipolar disorder; at this time, there is no known cure. Lithium is effective in *controlling* the disease, meaning that the person who sustains the appropriate dose is not likely to experience the symptoms. If a patient stops taking the medicine, there is a strong likelihood that the symptoms will recur.

Unlike with traditional antidepressants, periodic blood tests are needed when Lithium treatment is administered, especially in the early stages. Sometimes this may seem inconvenient, but it provides the doctor with an objective measurement to indicate if the proper dosage is being given.

Is the Use of Medicine an Admission of Weakness?

Let's go back to Richard, the man introduced at the beginning of the chapter who resisted Dr. Minirth's suggestion for medication. His attitude toward medicine reflects a very common reluctance encountered by virtually every mental health professional recognizing the occasional need for such a treatment.

Sure enough, some of Richard's problem with depression was tied to a history of poor emotional management. In his childhood, he had been trained in the "be tough" school of thought. When he displayed insecurity or anxiety, his father would readily lecture him about the nonsense of those reactions. He was told that his tensions were a show of weakness, and he was not allowed to be weak.

So did his emotional strains go away as he tried to fit the mold prescribed by his father? Of course not. Early in life he learned to hide his feelings, meaning they usually thrived "underground" and caused him to avoid the open process of resolving his tensions.

Do you have this same holdover from your history? What experiences taught you not to reveal or explore your emotions openly? (For instance, "My family was all business, and we just didn't take the time to discuss personal matters.")

_____

_____

_____

This trend continued throughout Richard's adulthood. Often irritable, sometimes insecure and defensive, he did not let many people into his inner world, preferring to follow his father's "be tough" approach to life. Many experiences created frustration and disappointment over the years, but he did such a poor job of addressing them that he became increasingly symptomatic in his emotional problems. Rather than being the cause of his depression, his struggle to respond to Annette's stroke was merely the final push that revealed his emotional difficulties.

By the time he sought help, he had been through years of stress and strain, to the extent that his body and mind were just worn out. The medicines were introduced not as the complete cure for his depression but as a relief for his physical symptoms. By correcting the physical aspects of his depression, *then* he could be freed to search out new and better ways to handle his conflicts and stresses.

As you look back upon your depression tendencies, what early signs showed that your emotions were taking a toll on your body? (For instance, "For years I've seemed to tire more easily than others.")

1. _____
2. _____
3. _____

If it is determined that medicines could help ease your physical symptoms, what emotional or relational habits would you then be freed to change? (For instance, "Once I return to normal sleep patterns, I'll be more able to manage the larger conflicts with my family," or "When I cease my weeping spells I'll be able to express my frustrations more constructively.")

1. _____
2. _____
3. _____

Remember that a goal of medicine is to relieve you of your most debilitating depressive symptoms, but once that is done you will find fullest relief from your depression as you use your rediscovered energy to tackle the deeper stressors that accompany your experience of depression.

11

Be Honest About
Suicidal Thoughts

Step 11. Reveal your struggles with thoughts about death. Allow others to know you thoroughly.

Depression has a way of draining people of their desire to live. If you have ever felt so down that you have longed to die, do not think of yourself as abnormal. You are merely wanting relief from pain, and that is legitimate. Understand, of course, that other means of pain relief are available, but the desire for something less burdensome is completely understandable.

When we encounter people who consider taking their lives, we have two immediate goals in mind: (1) Even though we know there are far better solutions than suicide, we want to communicate that the feelings associated with such thoughts can have reasonable roots; and (2) We want to introduce the availability of intervention so the suicidal thoughts eventually subside, leaving the individual free to tackle the causes of the problem.

Kristi was a thirty-two-year-old woman who had come to the end of her rope. When she first sought help from Dr. Carter she cried frequently and expressed little optimism that she could overcome her circumstances. Divorced and remarried, she was extremely disillusioned because her husband of one year was not the Sir Galahad she had hoped he would be. He was not abusive or unloving but neither was he the nurturing husband she had assumed she was getting. She had one child, a five-year-old son, and he was sometimes so hard to manage that her common response to his misbehavior was rage. It was after a major battle with the son, Jeremy, that she decided to seek help. She had bottomed out.

"I hate my life" was the first thing she said when Dr. Carter asked about her reason for seeking counseling. "Ever since I was a little girl I've struggled just to keep my sanity. I've had one setback after another, and I've learned not to feel optimistic about anything because it will only set me up for disappointment."

As a girl, Kristi felt unloved by her mother, who was a harsh disciplinarian. She found no comfort in her relationship with her father, who was nice but just not very available. She recalled numerous times when she had been severely reprimanded, leaving her feeling insecure and afraid. Though she had exhibited spunk and liveliness in her preteens, by her teenage years she had become increasingly reclusive. "I made a deliberate decision," she explained, "to lay low and take no chances. I had been thrown to the mat so many times that it just wasn't worth the effort to get back on my feet."

Marrying at nineteen to get away from her home life, she was quickly disillusioned by her new husband's selfishness and insensitivity. "He always had to have his way. We fought like cats and dogs until we finally had our fill of each other and divorced." Her second husband, George, was less severe in his anger, yet she felt that he too was not able to understand how to love her.

"Last week I had a miserable time trying to get my son to behave, and I just came completely unglued. When George came home, he told me to get a grip on life, which just sent me from bad to worse. I ran and locked myself in the bedroom and cried for nearly two hours. I've been very depressed before but never like that night. I had some medicine in the cabinet, and I came real close to swallowing it all. I wanted to die in the worst way!"

As Kristi retold this scene to Dr. Carter, she could not contain her tears. Sobbing deeply, she put her head into her hands, bent over in her chair, and said quietly, "I don't want to live any longer."

Have you ever felt like that? What experiences have brought about such a feeling? (For instance, "When I learned my mate had been unfaithful, I wanted to die," or "I've tried so hard to make friends, but my lack of success has drained me of my desire to live.")

_____

_____

_____

Before you dismiss your suicidal feelings as completely irrelevant, what is legitimate about some of the *feelings* you have experienced? (For instance, "It's legitimate that I dislike rejection," or "It's legitimate to want consistency from my family.")

_____

_____

_____

_____

Now, look more carefully at the thought of dying. What is *not* legitimate about it? (For instance, "It would mean that I have lost faith in my purpose for life, and I know God gave each person a purpose," or "I know people who would be seriously affected if I took my life.")

Dr. Carter sat quietly as Kristi cried. Then he spoke gently: "Kristi, I am very saddened by the fact that you have felt disillusioned in your major relationships. It's only natural that you would have high hopes regarding your relationship with your son and your husband." After a pause, he added, "I can promise you that if you'll let yourself be helped, we can get you through this crisis. Things may seem bleak now, but I am certain that you can find a new style of life if you commit to the process of change."

Suicidal depression is not hopeless. It *can* be only if the depressed person refuses intervention, but we have been part of numerous cases where people have come back from the deepest pit to live very satisfactory lives. In fact, sometimes the struggle with suicide represents a bottoming-out experience that serves as the necessary wake-up call prompting lasting change. Don't despair if you are in that low place!

Steps to Overcoming Suicidal Thinking

In order to get beyond the pain of suicidal thinking, you can take several steps. Pay careful attention to the thoughts expressed on the next few pages because they can literally save your life.

1. Openly admit your struggle.

A common problem that accompanies suicidal depression is a feeling of profound isolation. In most cases, depressed people have already attempted to reveal their tensions only to be disappointed in the response. For instance, Kristi had spoken to her sister about her long-standing insecurities, stemming back to childhood experiences. The sister, whose personality was considerably tougher, responded: "Look, I don't know why you have to whine about Mother's problems. She'll never change, so you're going to have to be the one to grow up!"

Was the sister wrong in what she told Kristi? Not entirely. But her response missed the point. Kristi had shared her feelings in the hope of receiving some validation, but instead she received a reprimand. Add to that the fact that her first husband had been completely out of touch with her needs and her second husband often felt overwhelmed by her emotions, and you can understand why she felt so isolated.

Has this ever happened to you? When have you attempted to share your emotional needs, only to feel disappointed? (For instance, "Once I tried to talk to a minister about my problems, but he was in a hurry and didn't really know what to say.")

_____

_____

_____

How did this experience leave you feeling? (For instance, "It seemed my needs didn't matter.")

_____

_____

_____

_____

You may attempt to signal others when you are sinking deeper into the pit of despair, but there is always the possibility that the one receiving the signal will not know what to do with it. Don't quit.

Not every person will know how to respond to your needs, but there *are* people who will want to help. Whether it is in a church setting or at work or within your family or in your circle of acquaintances, you can find someone who will lend a listening ear. Keep looking until you find that person.

If you are at the point of contemplating suicide, do not hesitate to seek out someone with professional skills to handle such a problem. There is no honor in trying heroically to carry the load by yourself. Furthermore, keeping your needs secret only allows them to grow in exaggerated proportions. For example, after telling Dr. Carter about her episode in which George chided her to "get a grip on life," Kristi admitted, "As I sit here telling you this, I realize that George was just as frustrated as me. He loves me and can't stand to see me in pain. He doesn't always know what to do with me, but it doesn't take away from the fact that he really cares."

Openly addressing your feelings and needs can generate objectivity. As you hear yourself enunciate your needs to someone else, you will often find yourself softening some of your harsher conclusions. For instance, as Kristi admitted George's love for her, it helped her realize that she was not the complete nobody she had been telling herself she was.

What adjustments in your thoughts might occur if you could speak clearly about your feelings to an understanding person? (For instance, "I'd probably have to admit that I'm not as helpless as I sometimes tell myself I am.")

_____

_____

_____

2. Believe that you can be helped.

Openness has a way of loosening the gloomy feelings you are experiencing, but for it truly to work you will need to be willing to be helped. When you have been depressed for several months or longer it is easy to lapse into such a pessimistic attitude that you may not be ready to be helped when help is finally available. For instance, one woman had been seriously depressed for more than five years and was finally persuaded to seek help at our clinic. After she gave Dr. Minirth the details of her problem, he asked her what she would like to accomplish in her therapy. Immediately her face went blank. Stammering, she replied, "I don't really know. I guess it never crossed my mind that I'd really be at a point of turning my depression around." Her statement summarizes the rut people can get stuck in when they have been dwelling at the bottom of the pit.

Depression has a way of becoming habitual, even when it is extremely distasteful. If you allow it, depression can feel so natural that contentment seems out of reach.

What experiences have you had that would indicate that you have grown too accustomed to your feelings of defeat? (For instance, "For the last year I've been very cynical even when people speak to me encouragingly.")

1. _____

_____

2. _____

_____

Let yourself be helped! See yourself as capable of something other than perpetual gloom! Circumstances may indeed be very disillusioning, but they do not have to be so debilitating that they leave you completely inert.

To be helped you will need to let go of your victim's mind-set. This is not to suggest that you have not been victimized by others' harshness or insensitivity, because in all likelihood you have. But it does mean that you can prompt yourself to look at something other than your miseries. Focusing too heavily on your victimization, you can become so anchored in bitterness and misery that they become the defining elements in your personality.

For instance, Kristi was *very* willing to speak at length when Dr. Carter asked about problems she had with her mother or her first husband. She would go on and on about how persistent her mother was in criticisms. She told numerous stories of episodes when her mother would embarrass her in front of friends or when she would fly into rages over small matters. She also could not emphasize enough how terribly her first husband treated her. He was a liar, unreliable, secretive, abusive. Clearly, Kristi had more than her fair share of miseries to recall.

But when the doctor asked, "What is good about you that you'd like others to see?" she would stammer for an answer. This weak reaction was somewhat understandable, given the fact that insecurity accompanies depression, but it also revealed something seriously wrong. Kristi was so geared to react to her miseries that complaining was all she knew. Here she was now speaking with a counselor who wanted to learn about her pluses, and she hardly knew what to say.

Has this ever happened to you? What signs indicate that you may be too engrossed in your experiences of victimization? (For instance, "I've been told by family members that I am constantly pessimistic.")

1. _____

2. _____

3. _____

Your problems are only a portion of your identity. Though you may not have learned to embrace your positives as fully as you might like, they are there nonetheless. Find them. Let others see them.

Dr. Carter prodded Kristi by reminding her, "I've noticed several times how pleasant you are when you speak to my secretary. Where does that come from?"

"Oh I can be that way to lots of people, but that's just my public face I put on."

"Not so fast! Don't be so ready to pass off that friendliness as an insignificant matter. I suspect if we took an inventory of the past twenty years we'd find hundreds of similar episodes. That is too common of a trait for you to brush off as merely a false front." He was able to get her to admit that several friends through the years found her easy to talk to. She could be very encouraging.

What positive traits do you have that have been inside you for a long time? (For instance, "I've never been a very overbearing person; I let people be what they are.")

1. _____

2. _____

3. _____

We are not suggesting that you deny your pain and tension. But in order for you to get beyond suicidal thoughts, you need reminders that you are more than the sum total of your problems. There is a legitimate foundation to be built upon. If others have rejected or abused you, it does not mean you cease to have a good core to your personality. Instead it probably means you are up against some hard-hearted people who have a vested interest in keeping you down.

Rather than interpreting rejection as meaning that you are beyond help, what other interpretations could you place on your circumstances? (For instance, "The fact that my husband quit loving me doesn't mean I am no longer lovable. Perhaps it shows how driven he is by his own selfish pursuits.")

_____

_____

_____

3. Accept responsibility for change.

Once you believe you can be helped, you will pass into a very important phase of recovery. You will cease wishing that others will be your caretakers, and you will take full responsibility for your own growth, whether or not others choose to support your efforts. This is unnatural for many people who are suicidally depressed because they have worked so long to get others' approval or permission to grow. Nevertheless, you will need to realize that no person is God. No one can play the role of rescuer. If growth happens, it will ultimately be the result of your own choices before God regarding the direction that is best.

When Dr. Carter talked with Kristi about this concept, she was initially stung by it, although she also knew he was speaking words she needed to hear. Her first reaction was "It almost sounds like you're telling me the same thing my sister said, that I can't just dwell in the memories of my mother's treatment toward me." But after a brief pause she spoke, "I don't get the sense, though, that you're rushing me through my problem or belittling the feelings I have had."

"Not at all," he replied. "I try to put myself into your shoes, and I think about how I would feel if I had had a lifetime of bossiness or criticism by my own mother. It would frustrate the daylights out of me just as it does you. Instead of this being a put-down, I am wanting you to accept a very real truth. Your desperate hope for someone to rescue you from your miseries has left you sorely disappointed. I fear that if you keep clinging to the assumption that *someone* has to be there to give you happiness, you could lose all optimism."

It is wonderful to find people who can be loving while you are hurting, and this is something you should do. Yet, you can simultaneously proceed with the notion that you are going to improve even if others are not currently on track with you. By incorporating the insights mentioned earlier in this book, by making behavioral adjustments, by communicating boundaries differently, you can learn to feel differently about yourself.

By taking responsibility for your own growth, you are presented with a bad news/good news situation. The bad news is that you cannot count on others to understand you so completely that they will rescue you from your depression. The good news is that you are free to make your own right choices about your life without having to filter them through others.

For instance, Dr. Carter explained, "Kristi, your most recent discouragement was prompted by your ongoing frustration regarding your son's temper flare-ups and your inability to make your husband respond to your liking. But let's look at it from a fresh angle. You can decide that, though it is nice to have your family members' cooperation, that is not going to be a mandatory requirement for your personal stability. You can practice what I call *delicate detachment* as you make it through your daily grind."

Delicate detachment means you will proceed with your own healthy plans for right living, and if others choose not to cooperate, that is their problem, not yours. For instance, notice some of the adjustments Kristi made:

1. When her son misbehaved, he was placed in time-out, and Kristi did not have to force him to like it or to feel good about her at the moment. She assumed that she could only do so much to make him act right. It was her job to monitor her own ability to act patiently.
2. She explained to her husband, George, how he could help her, but she also made room for the fact that he would not always

211

come through on her behalf. She was not going to let her expectations exceed his ability to make her feel calm.
3. She decided she needed a personal life away from her home life. She had always wanted to take tennis lessons, so she enrolled in a course at the community college for this purpose.

What about you? What are some situations in which you need to expect less from others and draw more from within yourself for satisfaction? (For instance, "I've always wanted my mother's approval for my child-rearing decisions, but it's *my* responsibility, not hers, to decide what is best for my family.")

1. _____
_____

2. _____
_____

List several adjustments you can make as you assume more responsibility for your emotional direction. (For instance, "I can quit trying to force my husband into discussions about personal issues he cares little about.")

1. _____
2. _____
3. _____

By taking responsibility for yourself, you are showing that you are not threatened by a crisis, that you see it as an incentive to make needed adjustments. People who stay in major depression usually do so because they are still wishing to force others to rescue them. People who grow because of their experience of depression do so because they see it as a signal that new courses need to be pursued . . . and they go after them!

4. Stay in touch with routine matters.

By the time Kristi sought help, she had cut herself off from people who in the past had been a good source of support. For instance, she no longer was involved in her activities at church. She had chosen to withdraw from her previous volunteer work at her son's school. She chose not to attend her son's soccer games because she did not want to see any of the other parents. She usually screened her phone calls with the answering machine so she would talk to people the least amount possible.

Dr. Carter explained, "The longer you cut yourself off from routine activities, the more difficult you will make it on yourself to get back into the swing of things. I totally understand the need to relax on some of the more pressing aspects of your life; you need a break in some areas. I just want to make sure you don't go so far in your withdrawal that you invite the very loneliness you are wanting to remedy."

Isn't it easy to take our stress reduction practices to the far extreme? Kristi *did* need to do a better job of taking care of her personal needs, yet she did not need to check out of life altogether, something she was dangerously close to doing.

Have you had this same problem? What legitimate self-protective measure have you taken to the far extreme? (For instance, "I needed to be less tied up with my extended family's problems, but now I don't even want to see them at major holidays.")

1. _____

2. _____

3. _____

Stay in touch with your routine life, even as you make corrections in your stress management. For instance, maybe you don't need to be on all those committees at church, but it doesn't mean you need to stop attending church altogether. Or perhaps you *do* need to stop getting so involved in the problems of your friends, but you don't need to cut yourself off from them completely.

> List some of your routines that you probably need to reestablish even as you are continuing to climb out of your depression. (For instance, "I could do more of the housework," or "I can still make calls to my friends to let them know I'm interested in them.")

1. _____
2. _____
3. _____
4. _____

Your depression indicates that you need to change some of your old patterns, but it does not mean that *everything* about your old way of life needs to be completely scrapped.

5. Be willing to seek intensive treatment if necessary.

In his early dealings with Kristi, Dr. Carter realized her depression was the result of a fairly long-standing problem (over six months) and that she needed a nudge to push her over the hump. Weekly outpatient counseling was not enough, given her desire to end her life. So for three weeks, at his recommendation, Kristi submitted to a more intensive day treatment program, headed by Dr. Minirth. For five days a week from 8:00 A.M. to 5:00 P.M., she received individual counseling, group counseling, educational sessions, and medical evaluations. The work was very focused and helped her get a clear perspective that could have taken months in outpatient treatment. During this time of day treatment, she was treated with antidepressant medicines, a common need for people who are suicidally depressed. Because of the severity of her depression she could not have recovered nearly as well without this approach.

After her completion of this intense program, she admitted to Dr. Carter, "At first I wasn't real sure if I should get the daily treatment because I was afraid it would be an admission of ultimate weakness. But then I realized I *was* weakened, so it only made sense to get the help I needed. I was pleasantly surprised to learn how supportive everyone was, from the therapists to the clerical staff to the other patients. The team atmosphere really pulled me through a rough time."

Several indicators would imply a need for the intensive approach as opposed to weekly outpatient therapy:

- persistence of depression symptoms even after good treatment has been sought

- the desire to die

- complications related to other medicines or physical ailments

- a near-complete inability to function as normal

- major social isolation

- feeling chronically overloaded by stress

- major physiological problems—ulcers, headaches, chronic fatigue, anorexia

- breaks from reality

- ongoing substance abuse

- behaviors that indicate poor impulse control, such as binge eating or other self-destructive behaviors

- inability to stop crying

- severe isolation accompanying depression

If you relate to even one or two of these indicators, you could be a good candidate for inpatient treatment, but if you can relate to five or more, it would be wise to consult soon with a therapist or medical doctor about the advisability of getting the help you need.

Be honest. What excuses might you use to postpone getting this kind of help? (For instance, "I wouldn't want my family to know," or "I couldn't get the time off from work.")

1. _____
2. _____
3. _____

Now for each excuse, what different perspective could you use? (For instance, "If my family knew about my depression, it would probably result in some needed open discussions," or "I can't afford to continue at work at my present low level of concentration.")

1. _____
2. _____
3. _____

Remember, we're talking about your life. Don't hesitate to get the treatment you need, and be thankful that it is as widely available as it is.

If You Know Someone Who Is Suicidal

Too often people can feel overwhelmed when they learn of someone's suicidal feelings, so they do what's easiest: They try to sweep the problem under the rug. "It's not that bad," they say. Or "Just don't let things get to you." The worst response is all too common, ignoring the problem altogether.

Don't let that happen when you learn that someone you know is struggling with such severe depression. You don't have to pretend you have all the answers, because even if you don't, you can help. Keep several ideas in mind:

1. Don't be afraid to talk about the problem.

Kristi told Dr. Carter, "I've learned that if I am bold enough to tell someone the extent of my feelings, they are blown away. You're the first person I know who has been willing to hear me out and want to learn more."

If you learn of a person's suicidal tendencies, ask questions:

• How long have you felt this way?

• Are you serious enough that you have devised a potential plan?

• What are you looking for that would help?

• What do you suppose has caused you to get to this point?

• What would you like me to know that would be helpful to you?

These types of questions indicate that you are interested and that you are able to be accepting even in the presence of an undesirable situation. In discussing the problem, the suicidal person can feel less isolated and therefore less likely to follow through.

If you are afraid that discussing the problem may only make matters worse, in most cases you are wrong. Usually, open discussion can help the depressed person become more objective. Hearing his or her own feelings expressed out loud can diminish the strength of emotion that can build when it is all held inside. Remember, talking about the problem doesn't mean you have to load the person up with unwanted advice. It means you are an accepting listener.

2. Encourage the suicidal person to get help.

Too often it is easy to assume that if you suggest counseling or psychiatric treatment, the depressed person will feel insulted. The first error in this thought is that it is condescending to suggest help. It is no more insulting to suggest professional help for someone experiencing major depression than it is for someone who has heart problems or a broken bone. Second, the depressed person has probably already considered getting treatment anyway. You will only be reinforcing a thought already there.

In a case of true suicidal possibility, it may be appropriate to enlist family or friends, making them aware of the severity of the problem. Although you want to be known as someone who can be entrusted with confidential and sensitive information, the potential of death overshadows the need for secrecy. In cases of imminent suicide, call an available doctor or an emergency medical unit.

3. When appropriate, share your own humanness.

A very pleasant by-product of our work with depressed patients is the opportunity to witness how relationships can deepen. Though it doesn't happen in all cases, we have known many depressed people who have told family or friends about their problems, and much deeper loving relations have developed.

For instance, several weeks after her day treatment program, Kristi attended a weekend women's retreat sponsored by her church. She took the risk of sharing the depths of her problems with several of the women there, and to her surprise she learned she was not the only one with similar problems. Two of the women, in particular, told about very similar feelings. They swapped stories, cried together, and prayed together. It was a tremendous uplifting experience that was very therapeutic for Kristi, not to mention the other women involved.

Can you be open with your own struggles as you learn about the problems of someone else? You need not hog center stage with your own revelations, but you can give comfort by letting the hurting person know of your own fallibility. No one is immune to the strains of emotional problems, so you would be injecting a major dose of reality into your relationship with a depressed person by revealing some of your humanness.

4. Check up on the suicidal person afterward.

Once you have learned of a person's suicidal tendencies, don't make it the last time to talk about it. Your initial discussion about the problem will probably be a major help, but there is always a chance the depression can return to the same low level. Follow-up can be a crucial way of saying: "I take you seriously."

Kristi revealed that after her disclosure at the women's retreat, one of the ladies made calls to her on a regular basis, averaging about once or twice a week. "I told her that I had gone so long feeling like I didn't belong that it was a tremendous shot in the arm for her to show the interest she did. I can honestly say she was a very helpful part of my recovery."

Suicidal depression is ultimately resolved by the person experiencing it. No one can make it go away for that person. That being the case, there is still much to be said on behalf of encouragers. The personality functions best when it is part of a supportive system of loving, caring people. Be certain you are a major part of that system.

12

Keys to Lasting Change

Step 12. Be committed to positive attitudes that can bring balance to your emotions.

In all of the preceding chapters we have built our thoughts on one major assumption: Depression can be understood and managed. It does not have to be a dark mysterious force that wreaks havoc in your life. You may not find depression an *easy* problem to confront, but it does not have to be an *impossible* problem.

Each of the patients we highlighted in this book had one thing in common as they sought help. They chose to take responsibility for their own growth, using awareness as the springboard to significant changes in thoughts, behaviors, and communications. What about you? Are you willing to sign on as someone who likewise is ready to do whatever it takes to break depression's hold in your life? The process may at times seem slow or unnatural, but it can happen!

In treating depression cases, we have found five keys that will keep you moving in the direction toward inner peace and composure. Consider each one carefully as we close out our study.

Key #1. It's not your job to make others change or understand.

Depression does not arise from a vacuum. The early symptoms of depression are virtually always tied to disappointing experiences involving major people in your life. You have been disappointed in someone's unwillingness to meet your legitimate needs. You have felt heartbroken in the loss of a major relationship. Your finances are strained. Your support system has broken down.

When these unwanted intrusions come into your life, it is very natural for you to think: "Who's going to get me away from these problems?" or "Why can't anyone understand how I feel?" or "Someone's got to provide me with some relief!"

Is it wrong to want outside help or understanding? Of course not. People function best when surrounded by a supportive, caring team.

But let's underscore a thought that may not feel too encouraging: If you are going to grow out of your depression, don't count on someone else's change or understanding. You may be in for a long wait! To change, start with the belief that change can happen even in the face of poor support from significant others. Your adjustments can be internally, not externally, motivated.

Go back to chapter 1 and recall Janice, the professional woman who seemingly had many good things going for her: a good career, solid community standing, the typical suburban lifestyle. Yet she suffered from depression because her husband, Wayne, was noncommunicative, because she had lost both parents in her twenties, because she couldn't say no to the many requests for her time.

Janice's depression was perpetuated by one major question: "When is anyone going to slow down long enough to consider *my* needs?"

In the course of therapy, she and Dr. Carter explored a wide range of issues related to the influence of her developmental years on her patterns of managing emotions, responding to hurt, pressuring herself to achieve. Because she had never taken the time to consider deeply these personal subjects, she found her sessions very stimulating and encouraging.

Yet, as time passed, Janice kept returning to one particularly sore subject. Her husband could not (or would not) understand her reasons for feeling depressed. "Every time I try to pull him into my world, he resists. He's not a bad guy, but nothing seems to move him. We're so detached!"

When Dr. Carter stated that she would need to continue her growth goals, with or without Wayne's understanding, she agreed and protested at the same time. "I know that's true, but it's so empty, knowing I have to move forward without his emotional awareness."

When have you had similar feelings of nonunderstanding? (For instance, "Recently I wrote my father a letter telling him about my feelings and my needs, and he acted as if he never read it.")

1. _____

_____

2. _____

_____

In Janice's case, she felt hopeless, angry, betrayed by Wayne's lack of insight. What similar reactions have you had? (For instance, "I've been ready to walk out of my relationship," or "I've been very temperamental.")

_____

_____

_____

Dr. Carter asked Janice a simple question, "Do you know the most frequently used word in marital arguments?" She shook her head no, so he continued, "It's the little word *you.*" She smiled as she had to admit that certainly was the case in her home.

"I want you to get to the point where you'll put much less emphasis on his need to change and more emphasis on the one person you can do something about, *yourself.*"

He had Janice list several positive adjustments she could make even in spite of her husband's lack of input. For instance:

• Though his cooperation would be helpful, she acknowledged that she could still manage to speak her anger productively instead of holding it in as she normally did.

• She could branch out with efforts to strengthen friendships with peers she had always wanted to know better.

• She would set better boundaries regarding time management.

• When her husband became bossy or critical, she would determine not to be so controlled by him that she could not pursue her own good decisions.

What are some positive changes you can make in your life even when you cannot force others to change with you? (For instance, "I can speak with confidence to my extended family even when I know they will be skeptical," or "I could take more initiative in scheduling social activities.")

1. _____

2. _____

3. _____
4. _____

Let's acknowledge that, though it is ideal to grow and mature with close companions moving alongside you, your personal stability is too important to let it hinge on someone else's lack of effort. Doggedly determine that you'll not let people dictate your personal goals.

Key #2. Lifelong changes begin with daily adjustments.

It's easy to approach a subject like depression with a theoretical or philosophical approach. You can learn all the whys of depression, becoming full of textbook information, but until you learn to channel that knowledge into daily application, you are merely chasing the wind.

Suppose, for instance, you learn that your depression persists because you have come under too many controlling influences. It's good to be aware of the effects of control on your emotions, but are you making any specific changes? Or perhaps you'll admit that your depression is directly tied to long-standing struggles with insecurity, meaning you need to revamp your thoughts about yourself. That's good, but have you taken it to the next level? That is, are your new thoughts directly influencing behavior?

Dr. Carter wanted Janice to be very specific as she made inroads into her problem with depression. For instance, she admitted that in spite of her history of good grades and career achievement, she had hidden feelings of insecurity. Few people knew this about her. So he stated, "You're painting yourself into a very uncomfortable corner by holding on to those negatively charged thoughts about yourself. We've been discussing a new perspective about your God-given self-worth, and you seem to be absorbing that perspective well. What daily adjustments can we expect to see based on your new thinking?"

"Well, I guess I could be more open with people about myself. I could take more chances in my self-revelations."

"That's a good thought," replied the doctor. "But let's be more specific. Who will you be more open with, and how will it be shown in your daily routine?"

Janice was good at intellectualizing her need for change, but she realized Dr. Carter was wanting to be more than a professor to her. She thought for a moment, then said, "Well, when I go home in the evenings, Wayne has this typical routine of reading books or talking on the phone while basically ignoring me. I could do a better job of insisting on having some time where we pay better attention to each other. I think he'd be receptive to that."

As her counseling progressed, Janice learned that often her problem was not one of ignorance or intention but of follow-through. She wanted to feel more secure with Wayne, meaning she felt it would be important to initiate time to share and connect. Yet, it was easy to think: "Tomorrow I'll get to it," or "I'll wait for him to show an interest first." She learned, though, that she would make greater inroads into her recovery if she could pinpoint *how* to put her insights into action.

Notice some common illustrations of ways you can be specific regarding your daily growth goals:

- As you recognize your tendency to say yes to your coworkers' unreasonable requests, determine to specifically pinpoint the requests you can say no to.

- Instead of pleading with or coaxing your child to do her homework promptly, set a system of clear consequences this afternoon for the choices she makes regarding her schedule.

• Knowing you need not defend yourself in the face of your father-in-law's frequent criticisms, determine that this Saturday's outing with him will contain no defensive statements.

What are some specific behaviors you can practice that will illustrate that your knowledge is truly making a difference in your life? (For instance, "At my next social event, I will be very deliberate to include myself in conversations with John and Sue.")

1. _____
_____

2. _____
_____

Let's take this concept one step further. You can gain even greater focus by specifying your behavioral adjustments to particular times of the day. For instance, if you know that mornings are commonly wasted as you mope with no direction, you can decide to take from 9 o'clock to 11 o'clock once a week to do your grocery shopping. A team of wild horses won't stop you. Or, if you are not very assertive when you attend your company's weekly organizational meetings, you can declare to yourself that during that meeting between 1 o'clock and 2 o'clock you will clearly discuss the needs of your job. By being time-specific, your ideas become more pertinent.

When are some common times that you could specify definite adjustments in action? (For instance, "On weeknights right after supper I need to be very specific with my husband regarding the ways he can help with the kids.")

1. _____
_____

2. _____

_____

Key #3. Make yourself accountable.

We have found in working with depressed people that it is often easy for those people to feel temporarily motivated to change, only to have that motivation wear off rapidly as pessimistic thoughts take over. The mind of a depressed person is easily slanted toward pessimism anyway, so once that person sets down the self-help book or spends a day or two away from the motivation of the counselor's office, it is easy to think: "It won't work." Don't think of yourself as abnormal if this happens to you.

Can you think of an experience when you were really charged up regarding change but then talked yourself out of following through with it? (For instance, "Last week I heard a great sermon on being confident, but by the next day I was back to my same old insecure self.")

_____

_____

_____

Though you cannot count on others to push you into the changes you need to make, you can nonetheless make use of trusted relationships to keep you motivated. Talk to a friend or a confidant specifically about your positive plans, and tell that friend that you'd welcome follow-up conversations in the days ahead.

One major admission that Janice made to Dr. Carter was that she rarely told people what she wanted to do to improve her life because she did not want to be guilty of empty speculating. But a break-through came when she began sharing some of her adjustment plans with her sister. For instance, Janice told her sister one Monday that she needed to scale down her schedule to prevent feelings of burnout. The next weekend her sister asked about the trimming she had made in her time commitments. Janice had made none, and she said to her sister, "I didn't really expect you to lean on me regarding my personal problems."

The sister explained, "I'm not going to lean on you in the sense of *forcing* you to do something against your will. But I agreed with you when you told me about your schedule overload, and I know you well enough to know you're too likely just to complain with no action. I love you enough to confront you about following through with what you said!"

Janice was fortunate that she had a sister who cared enough to keep her accountable. Knowing that someone was caringly watching her moves, Janice felt a much stronger inclination to do what she knew she needed to do.

> Are you willing to put yourself under accountability to someone you respect? What plan would you reveal to that person? (For instance, "I could tell my best friend about my willingness to work on softening my sharp tone of voice toward my family.")

_____

_____

_____

In the case of Janice's sister, the sister was assertive enough to call her on the carpet for being all talk and no action. You may be fortunate to have friends who will be firm with you when needed. But that may not necessarily be the case. Even so, you have at least two options with your accountability partner:

1. You can openly ask that person to speak to you honestly about what he or she sees in you that needs adjusting. Ask specific

questions: "How does my insecurity display itself when I'm with Sally?" or "Coach me regarding how I could have handled my conflict with my husband; what blind spots do I seem to have?"

2. You can share your growth goals with an accountability partner; then immediately make specific plans to get back in touch after a reasonable period of time. For instance, after telling a friend how you will behave less passively during your next get-together with those difficult family members, declare: "I'm going to call you after I get home and tell you about my improved mannerisms."

By openly discussing your feelings and plans with an accountability partner, you are not necessarily nursing an unhealthy dependency relationship (although it could become that if you have to report in too frequently). Instead, let's acknowledge that most people tend to be at their best when they realize that significant persons are on the sidelines pulling for them. Solid accountability can generate needed encouragement.

How could you benefit by making yourself more accountable? (For instance, "By talking more openly, I'd be less prideful and more likely to admit to myself the urgency for real change.")

_____

_____

_____

Key #4. Make allowances for setbacks.

Dr. Minirth sat across the desk from a woman as she wept and explained, "I just don't understand what has happened to me. I thought everything was going so much better, but now I'm feeling just as frustrated as ever." Lucy had spent three weeks at the clinic's day treatment program where she had undergone intensive treatment all day long, five days each week. During that time she had discovered the need for antidepressant medical intervention and had found major relief with the drug. Also, she had decided to be fully honest and open with her counselors and had gained significant insights into the reasons for her emotional breakdown. Upon leaving the program, she felt an optimism she had not experienced in years.

Now, a month later she explained to the doctor, "I knew things wouldn't become wonderfully rosy for me after I got back into my normal routine, but I just wasn't ready for what was going to happen." Her depression had deep roots in a long-standing tension between herself and her father. During her time of treatment she had some healing conversations with him and was able to rethink some old problems of shame and guilt and anger.

"Two days ago," she elaborated, "I was visiting my parents, and Dad was very cold toward me. He didn't say anything derogatory, but he just ignored me. I had just gotten used to the idea that we were on better terms when he pulled this stunt. It really frustrated me, but when I asked him to talk with me about his feelings, he had very little to say."

That disappointing interchange made Lucy doubt the improvements she had made in the previous two months. "Maybe he was just humoring me all along," she thought. "It's too optimistic to think I could actually have the relationship I want with him."

Has this ever happened to you? When have you dared to feel optimistic only to be let down by problems you thought were behind you? (For instance, "I've decided that I can have a few good conversations with my spouse, but sure enough it will return to the same old emptiness," or "I'm angrier now than I've ever been, and I don't care who knows about it.")

1. _____
   _____

2. _____
   _____

Virtually no one recovering from depression will experience smooth and steady adjustments. Instead, recovery usually follows the three-steps-forward, two-steps-backward route.

Setbacks in your healing do not indicate that all of the healing is lost, nor do they necessarily mean you are making wrong decisions. It is easy to interpret setbacks as failures when instead they are reminders of the inevitable frustrations that come with being an imperfect human who interacts daily with other imperfect humans.

For instance, Dr. Minirth explained to Lucy, "Your father's cool attitude can remind you that he may never be consistent in responding to you the way you'd like. Remember, the adjustments you're hoping for are very unnatural to him. He's not working as hard as you to be insightful so it's no shock that he would demonstrate old tendencies from time to time."

The doctor encouraged her to interpret her setback less severely. For instance, rather than seeing her father's aloofness as proof of her lowly status, she could interpret it more accurately as proof of his discomfort with sustained closeness. She needed to make room for such occurrences as she remembered that she, not he, was the one who was putting out the effort to change. Her inconsistency was predictable.

What less devastating interpretations could you put on your setbacks? (For instance, "When I feel myself withdrawing from my family again, I can interpret it as a legitimate need for private contemplation rather than assuming I'm permanently going back into a hole.")

_____

_____

_____

In order to prevent shock regarding potential setbacks, you may need to anticipate some of the undesirable occurrences you'll need to look out for. That way, you'll be less likely to feel like a failure.

What potential setbacks might you prepare for? (For instance, "I know my spouse won't be as enthusiastic about deeper communication as I am," or "It's likely that people at work will still want extra performance from me even when I clearly establish my new boundaries.")

_____

_____

_____

Two potential hindrances need to be openly admitted as you press forward toward personal improvements:

1. You are not likely to maintain a high level of energy and motivation at all times. There will be moments when you will feel like quitting, or at least taking a break from recovery. Don't let this surprise you.
2. Many people you interact with will make no changes or few changes. Some people simply do not care how their behavior affects you. This means you may experience feelings of rejection or hurt that you had hoped could be reduced. You'll need to base your growth on the assumption that this is a very real possibility.

What weaknesses or imperfections (in yourself or in others) will you need to allow for as you continue to change? (For instance, "I'm still shy in large groups," or "My temper is something I'll have to monitor carefully," or "My brother will never react sensitively to my moods.")

_____

_____

_____

_____

Your awareness of these potential hurdles will cause you to feel less defeated when they inevitably happen.

Key #5. See emotional healing as part of your spiritual awakening.

Underlying all we have said so far is the belief that depression can be managed only as you revamp the inner elements that define your self. For example, by choosing to handle your anger in ways that benefit both your own personal needs and those of others, you would be operating on the belief that you are someone of worth who believes in relationships anchored in mutual respect. Your inner thoughts direct your outer behavior.

Attention to your inner, spiritual self is implied in all aspects of depression treatment. Change just for the sake of change will get you nowhere. But change founded in spiritual convictions can be lasting.

Your depression indicates that you have lost your spiritual vitality. But you can get back on track as you come to terms with some thought-provoking questions:

• What is your purpose as you encounter people each day?

• What does it mean to be yielded to God?

- Where does a personal commitment to Jesus Christ fit into emotional management?

- How does knowing that God has a plan for your heavenly destination affect your daily decisions?

- Why would you want to commit to love or forgiveness or humility?

- How can your understanding of God's grace impact you as you face harsh realities of emotional pain or rejection?

- In what way are you meant to be a conduit to show godliness to others?

When you come to terms with questions like these, you can realize that your existence does not have to be defined by the outer world. Contemplate your Creator. Choose to rest in the belief that your life has meaning because it is God Himself who placed you on this earth.

What hindrances have kept you from being fully anchored in spiritual beliefs? (For instance, "I have been disillusioned by the religious crowd," or "I'd rather find my happiness in things more concrete.")

_____

_____

_____

To deepen your spiritual roots, you will have to be more of a thinker, less of a reactor. Not only would you not mind the challenge of grappling with questions regarding your meaning in life, you would welcome it.

What spiritual truths do you believe could make a real difference in your emotional stability? (For instance, "Seeing the enormity of creation, I know there is a God who has a master plan for my life," or "Jesus Christ is too real for me to ignore His teachings.")

1. _____

2. _____

3. _____

In speaking with people like Janice and all the others mentioned in this book, we are committed to reminding them that other people are not God. We live in a fallen, sin-stained world where it is absolutely predictable that people will fail. Only God is God. For a time, He is allowing sin to run its course here on Planet Earth, yet his eternal truths are still eminently applicable, and we can live with the assurance that He will bless His own with current peace and strength and future bliss and relief.

Don't approach your spiritual life as if it is purely a system of rules and regulations. That will defeat you quicker than anything. See spirituality as a personal relationship with God, provided for you by Christ, interpreted to you by the Holy Spirit.

You can find emotional stability as you incorporate beliefs like the following:

- My life is no accident. God can use me to demonstrate His strength and His love.

- I will care for myself as part of my commitment to receive God's love.

- Humility and forgiveness are cornerstone elements in my personality.

- When others fail me, God will not. He never ignores me.

You will find that as you strengthen your inner resolve to be guided by God, your emotions (though still susceptible to ups and downs) will be kept from the far extremes.

You *can* manage your depression.

Other Books in the
Minirth Meier New Life Clinics Series

Anger Workbook
Dr. Les Carter, Dr. Frank Minirth

Broken Vows
Dr. Les Carter

The Complete Life Encyclopedia
Dr. Frank Minirth, Dr. Paul Meier,
Stephen Arterburn

Day by Day: Love Is a Choice
Dr. Richard and Jerilyn Fowler,
Drs. Brian and Deborah Newman

Don't Let Jerks Get the Best of You
Dr. Paul and Jan Meier

Every Other Weekend
Kenneth Parker, Van Jones

The Father Book
Dr. Frank Minirth, Dr. Brian
Newman, Dr. Paul Warren

Free to Forgive
Dr. Paul Meier, Dr. Frank Minirth

The Headache Book
Dr. Frank Minirth

"Honey, Are You Listening?"
Dr. Richard and Jerilyn Fowler

Hope for the Perfectionist
Dr. David Stoop

Imperative People
Dr. Les Carter

The Intimacy Factor
Dr. David Stoop, Jan Stoop

Intimate Encounters
Dr. David and Teresa Ferguson,
Dr. Chris and Holly Thurman

Intimate Moments Daily Devotions
Dr. David and Teresa Ferguson,
Dr. Chris and Holly Thurman

The Lies We Believe
Dr. Chris Thurman

Love Hunger Action Plan
Dr. Sharon Sneed

*Love Hunger: Recovery from
Food Addiction*
Dr. Frank Minirth, Dr. Paul Meier,
Dr. Robert Hemfelt, Dr. Sharon
Sneed

*The Love Hunger
Weight-Loss Workbook*
Dr. Frank Minirth, Dr. Paul Meier,
Dr. Robert Hemfelt, Dr. Sharon
Sneed

Love Is a Choice
Dr. Robert Hemfelt, Dr. Frank
Minirth, Dr. Paul Meier

Love Is a Choice Workbook
Dr. Robert Hemfelt, Dr. Frank
Minirth, Dr. Paul Meier, Dr. Brian
Newman, Dr. Deborah Newman

My Infant
Dr. Paul Warren

My Preschooler
Dr. Paul Warren

My Toddler
Dr. Paul Warren

One Step at a Time
Cynthia Humbert, Dr. Frank Minirth,
Betty Lively Blaylock

Pace Yourself
Ric Engram

Passages of Marriage
Dr. Frank and Mary Alice Minirth,
Drs. Brian and Deborah Newman,
Dr. Robert and Susan Hemfelt

About the Authors

Dr. Frank Minirth is cofounder of the Minirth Meier New Life Clinics, one of the largest mental health care providers in the United States. He is a diplomate of the American Board of Psychiatry and Neurology and received an M.D. degree from the University of Arkansas.

Dr. Minirth has coauthored more than 30 books, including *The Power of Memories, The Headache Book, Love Is a Choice, Love Hunger, The Father Book, Things That Go Bump in the Night, The Anger Workbook, The Path to Serenity, Worry-Free Living, Happiness Is a Choice,* and *You Can!* He resides in Plano, Texas, with his wife and five daughters.

Dr. Les Carter is a nationally known expert in the field of Christian counseling, with more than eighteen years in private practice. He is a psychotherapist with the Minirth Meier New Life Clinics and is a guest on the clinic's popular daily radio program.

Dr. Carter earned his B.A. from Baylor University and his M.Ed. and Ph.D. from North Texas State University. He is the author or coauthor of more than twelve books, including *The Anger Workbook, Imperative People, Reflecting the Character of Christ,* and *Broken Vows.* Dr. Carter and his family reside in Dallas, Texas.